IMAGES
of America

JEWISH COMMUNITY
OF HARTFORD

IMAGES
of America

JEWISH COMMUNITY
OF HARTFORD

Jewish Historical Society
of Greater Hartford

ARCADIA
PUBLISHING

Copyright © 2016 by Jewish Historical Society of Greater Hartford
ISBN 978-1-4671-1596-4

Published by Arcadia Publishing
Charleston, South Carolina

Printed in the United States of America

Library of Congress Control Number: 2015950536

For all general information, please contact Arcadia Publishing:
Telephone 843-853-2070
Fax 843-853-0044
E-mail sales@arcadiapublishing.com
For customer service and orders:
Toll-Free 1-888-313-2665

Visit us on the Internet at www.arcadiapublishing.com

*This book is dedicated to the past, present, and future
Jewish community of Hartford, Connecticut.*

CONTENTS

ACKNOWLEDGMENTS

At one time, more than 13 synagogues and congregations supported a vibrant and growing community in Hartford. These first Jewish settlers made significant contributions to the city's economic growth and cultural diversity. They later followed a path from the city to the suburbs, as many early immigrants did in similar mid-sized cities. Their dedicated efforts and remarkable accomplishments laid the foundation for the active Greater Hartford Jewish community today, which continues to leave a sustaining legacy for the future.

Collecting and documenting Jewish life in Hartford is the primary focus of the Jewish Historical Society of Greater Hartford (JHSGH). The JHSGH Archives consist of more than 100 subject collections, over 5,000 photographic images, and more than 3,000 oral history interviews. Compiling over 200 archival images in preparation for this volume demonstrates the importance of preserving our communal history. By telling our pictorial story and creating community awareness of this unique material, we hope to provide a greater understanding of our community's culture and heritage for present and future generations.

The material for this publication was prepared by the society's committed staff who worked on this project for over a year. Archivist Sara Hawran collected, organized, and researched the selected images. Project manager Beatrice Brodie researched and wrote the captions. Archival intern Jeanne Lowrey assisted with the research. We are very grateful to our proofreaders: Ann Brandwein, Dr. Leon Chameides, Lance Goldberg, Jeanne Lowrey, Sandra Rulnick, and Susan Viner. In addition, we thank JHSGH president, Sandra Rulnick, and the board of directors for their ongoing support of the organization's projects, programs, and publications. To learn more, please visit www.jhsgh.org.

Unless otherwise specified, all photographs are courtesy of the Jewish Historical Society of Greater Hartford. All locations mentioned are in Hartford, Connecticut, unless otherwise noted.

—Estelle Kafer, JHSGH executive director

INTRODUCTION

The earliest known European to arrive in what would become Hartford was Adriaen Block, a Dutch explorer who established a fort near the merger of the Connecticut and Park Rivers in 1614. Dutch control was limited, however, and had little impact on the first English settlers (led by Protestant Congregational minister Thomas Hooker) who founded a permanent settlement in Newtown in 1635.

Not only was the Congregational Church supported by public taxes in the colony, but citizens were required to attend religious services. For nearly two centuries, the Congregational Church controlled much of Connecticut's religious, political, and social life. It did not welcome other Christian denominations or Jews. In 1818, the Connecticut constitution disestablished the Congregational Church and allowed other Christian groups to manage their own churches.

The earliest mention of Jews in Hartford comes from court and town meeting records. Among them were David the Jew (1659), an itinerant peddler, and Jacob the Jew (1667), a horse dealer. By 1788, advertisements in the *Hartford Courant* for stores located on "Jew Street"—most likely at the east end of State Street—began to appear.

Because of the strict limitations on their practice of religion, the few Jews who settled permanently in Connecticut did not form cohesive groups or establish permanent Jewish communities. Instead, they blended into the mainstream, frequently leaving their Jewish heritage behind.

By 1820, Hartford's population numbered about 6,000, mostly from English and Scottish backgrounds. The oldest neighborhoods were located between Main Street and the Connecticut River, Hartford's economic lifeline to the outside world.

Beginning with the advent of steam, which powered both boats and trains and provided fuel for industry, immigrants from different countries moved into the Main Street area. The earliest large group came from Ireland. The animosity directed towards Irish Catholics may have absorbed some of the prejudice that might have been aimed at the next group: German speakers.

By 1840, the population of Hartford had increased to 12,793, and the economy was robust, with jobs both in industry and its smaller suppliers. With the increasing population, there was also a need for services that supported the workers themselves in culturally appropriate ways. Hartford, in the center of the region with access to inexpensive transportation, was an excellent location for retail and business.

Fleeing political, economic, social, and religious (mainly for Jews) hardship and a general lack of progress, a large wave of immigrants, which included Jews, began to arrive from the various German principalities and Austria in the 1830s. This first permanent group of approximately 200 German Jews established the basis for today's modern Jewish community. Overall, the immigrants were eager to move into the mainstream and frequently wrote letters home inviting friends and relatives to join them in the growing city.

Among the newcomers were merchants, grocers, watch repairers, hotel owners, tanners, cattle dealers, and owners of small businesses. While some found jobs similar to those in the old country, others either adapted their skills to fit the new context or changed completely. A small group continued working in their religious professions. Although many only eked out a living, others prospered and became wealthy community leaders.

Forbidden by laws—rooted in the early dictates of the Congregational Church and upheld by the 1818 constitution—Jews in the early 1840s could not organize formal congregations. It was not until 1843 that groups from Hartford (that would become Congregation Beth Israel) and New Haven (Congregation Mishkan Israel) successfully petitioned to be allowed the same religious rights as Christians. However, neither this petition nor the 1868 adoption of the 14th Amendment to the US Constitution—the free exercise of religion clause—changed the Connecticut constitution to reflect complete freedom of religion. It was not until 1965 when restrictions on Jews were officially eliminated.

Within a few years of the arrival of the German Jews, the community had hired a rabbi, a *hazzan* (cantor), and a *shochet* (ritual slaughterer) and opened a religious school. The Ararat Lodge, a chapter of the national fraternal order of B'nai B'rith for men and the Frauen Verein, later called the Deborah Society, for women provided places where their members could gather for social events based on the culture and language of the old country. They also served as charitable and service organizations.

Beth Israel's earliest members first met in private homes. As their numbers increased, they moved to a larger rental space. In 1856, Beth Israel purchased the First Baptist Church building on the corner of Main and Temple Streets and renamed it Touro Hall after Judah Touro, the New Orleans philanthropist.

When Touro Hall was remodeled in 1865, Rabbi Isaac Mayer Wise, leader of the national Reform movement, came from Cincinnati for the rededication. In 1875, after fire destroyed part of the building, the congregation sold the property and purchased a lot on Charter Oak Avenue south of the immigrant neighborhood, near the large imposing homes of prosperous Yankees.

The Romanesque Revival building, designed by prominent architect George Keller, opened with a major ceremony in 1876 as the first synagogue built specifically for that purpose in Connecticut. Costing $35,567, the main hall seated 500. Although Beth Israel began as a German Orthodox synagogue, over time, members became less traditional, officially affiliating with the Reform Union of American Hebrew Congregations in 1878. Among the innovations were a choir with women (and later an organ), family seating, and group confirmations, replacing individual Bar Mitzvahs. Although these changes caused dissension among members, the majority embraced American Reform practices in keeping with the more liberal, secular attitudes that their founders had brought from Europe.

Between 1840 and 1880, the German-Jewish community entered a period of community growth and Americanization. Many spoke English, increasingly made connections with the mainstream Protestant community, and began to participate in public and political life. By the early 1880s, the population of Hartford stood at about 50,000, with about 1,500 Jews. But this would soon change.

The assassination of Russian Tsar Alexander II in 1881 inaugurated a combination of *pogroms* (mob violence against the Jews) and anti-Semitic May Laws, which limited every aspect of Jewish life in the Russian Empire. For the following 40 years, the increasingly difficult living conditions for Jews, coupled with three wars fought mostly in the Pale of Settlement (the western provinces of the Russian Empire including parts of Poland, where Jews were required to live), set in motion a population shift and migration that would affect not only the Jewish communities there, but also around the world.

In Hartford, the German Jews, who were in the process of blending into the mainstream, were uncomfortable with this large group of Jewish immigrants so different from themselves. The newcomers were almost uniformly poor, did not speak German, had little secular education, and practiced more traditional religious customs.

By 1910, the Jewish population in Hartford had increased to about 6,500, with the Jews sharing the Front Street neighborhood primarily with Italian Catholics. Almost everyone lived in tenements where conditions were crowded and unsanitary. Even so, it was an improvement over Europe, with its poverty and religious, economic, social, and political discrimination.

A primary value among Hartford's immigrant Jews was education. After work, adults studied English and civics in preparation for citizenship tests. Children attended public schools, where parents trusted the teachers to teach without overt anti-Semitism. Religious or secular Yiddish *folkschule* classes were relegated to after-school programs.

The Russian Jews entered the economy at many points. Some started as peddlers with the goal of moving up to pushcarts and from pushcarts to small businesses. Storefronts, kosher restaurants, and pharmacies offered additional types of economic opportunities and services. Windsor and Front Streets became the center for all sorts of immigrant commerce and social life, with the pushcarts drawing shoppers from throughout the city.

Hartford was a growing city, with jobs in construction and the building trades. Some Jewish tradesmen went on to become contractors and builders, hiring others to do the labor. New to the Hartford economy were Jewish furriers and cabinet makers. With politics virtually an Irish monopoly, only a few Jews ran for public office, primarily as Democrats from the immigrant districts.

Because Hartford's two hospitals—the Protestant Hartford Hospital and the Catholic Saint Francis Hospital—denied privileges to Jewish doctors, in 1918, a group of these doctors and community leaders began to discuss the need for a Jewish hospital. Five years later, in 1922, Mount Sinai Hospital opened, providing a place where Jewish patients would be comfortable and where Jewish doctors could practice.

In contrast to the established German Jewish view that the Eastern European Jews were a homogeneous religious mass, there was enormous diversity within the group. Since few were comfortable with Beth Israel's Reform practices, they set out to organize Orthodox synagogues that were reminiscent of home. Ados Israel (formerly Congregation of the Associated Brothers, Children of Israel), founded in 1884, was the first Orthodox synagogue to open. Between 1893 and 1919, groups founded 13 small Orthodox synagogues, all based on their countries of origin and their specific religious traditions. In 1919, another group organized the first Conservative synagogue, B'nai Israel, which became The Emanuel Synagogue.

Part of Jewish tradition has always been the importance of maintaining a strong, supportive community. Members took on the responsibility of caring for each other and for their less fortunate relatives overseas. They founded an orphanage, an old people's home, and a boarding house for transients who needed kosher food, and many other small institutions, all colored by their political and religious stances and the places and customs they had come from (Poland versus Romania, small town versus city). They organized political groups, *landsmanschaften* (organizations based on hometowns in Europe), mutual aid societies, cultural and educational clubs, and programs for all ages, Zionist organizations promoting a Jewish homeland, and burial societies. In 1912, thirty independent charities—including those founded by the German Jews—organized into a single association, the United Jewish Charities, the forerunner of the current Jewish Federation of Greater Hartford, which was established in 1945.

With immigration severely restricted by federal law after the mid-1920s, the Jews turned to community building. During the 1920s and 1930s, many began moving out of the downtown immigrant neighborhood to the North End—the Albany Avenue/Blue Hills Avenue area—where a vibrant American-Jewish community was developing.

The earliest transplants lived in the large apartment houses not far from downtown. Later, many moved farther north and west where builders were constructing two-, three-, and single-family homes. As their circumstances improved, many Jews moved around in this neighborhood; from apartment buildings to two- or three-family houses to private homes and from the east side of Keney Park to the more affluent west side and—sometimes, during the Depression—back again.

The children attended school with children from other groups who lived in the neighborhood. Many Jewish teenagers went to Weaver High School, where they generally had what was considered a good American experience. Many of the boys, in particular, went on to college and became professionals or businessmen.

The synagogues and other Jewish institutions soon followed their members out of downtown. While some closed, new groups emerged, and old ones evolved to meet the needs of the changing community.

In the 1930s, the rise of the Nazi Party in Germany led to a new concern: the rescue of the German Jews. With the Immigration Restriction Acts of the 1920s seriously limiting the flow of refugees into the United States, families found it very difficult to obtain visas for their relatives in Germany. Even so, both before and after the war, Hartford Jews fought to bring in the refugees.

The Jewish Family Service in Hartford helped resettle the pre-war refugees to some extent, but jobs were scarce during the Depression, and the newcomers had to take whatever was available. This wave of immigration ended in 1939 when the war in Europe began, and did not resume until after the war, when the United States admitted a relatively small number of displaced Jews.

Almost all of those coming after the war had suffered terribly, and some found it very difficult to adjust to America. People took whatever jobs they could find and worked hard despite, in many cases, their poor physical and/or mental health. The children in both groups of World War II refugees moved into the Hartford schools and learned English. Many went on to higher education and successful careers.

Although some Jewish families had left the North End for the suburbs in the 1930s, the true exodus did not begin until after World War II, as part of a national trend toward suburban life. As the Jewish population relocated, the synagogues, social service agencies, clubs, and recreational facilities followed them, in this case, primarily to West Hartford. The final push out of the North End—the inner city riots of the late 1960s—came after most of the Jewish population was gone, although some who still owned business were hurt by the fires and looting. These forces combined effectively broke up the dense Jewish area and scattered the Jews throughout the new neighborhoods.

During the final quarter of the 20th century, approximately 1,500 to 2,000 Soviet Jewish refugees arrived in Hartford. From the beginning, the Union of Soviet Socialist Republics had made life difficult for all Soviet citizens but particularly so for the Jews who faced special discrimination. However, with both emigration from the USSR and immigration to the United States restricted after the mid-1920s, the Jews had few options at that time.

In the 1960s, after the United States relaxed its immigration laws to allow refugees from Communism, Soviet Jews began to demand exit permits. Within 10 years, following a long political struggle, with the United States and Israel pressing for the release of the Jews, the Soviets began allowing a few to leave, with the first families arriving in Connecticut in the late 1970s.

Most Soviet Jews settled in West Hartford—at least temporarily. Unlike their predecessors, they received extensive help from the organized Jewish community. Overall, those coming to Hartford were highly educated and accustomed to the modern industrial world. Although it was difficult for many to enter and rise in the work force, most eventually did so. Their goal was to become Jews in America—according to their own definition—and to move into the same middle and professional class positions that they had achieved at home.

By the end of the 20th century, few Jews remained in Hartford. In 1989, the same year that the Hebrew Home left the city for its new facility in West Hartford, Mount Sinai Hospital, which had served the needs of both the Jewish community and the larger neighborhood for more than 70 years, negotiated an alliance with Saint Francis Hospital and Medical Center. With the merger complete in 1995, Mount Sinai, the last of the Jewish institutions in the city, ceased to operate under Jewish auspices. However, the Greater Hartford Jewish community, estimated to be about 32,000 in 2012, has flourished with synagogues, schools, social service agencies, and the Jewish Federation of Greater Hartford maintaining a strong presence in the surrounding communities.

—Betty N. Hoffman, PhD

Betty N. Hoffman is an anthropologist/oral historian specializing in the study of Jewish life in Connecticut. Her books are available through the Jewish Historical Society of Greater Hartford.

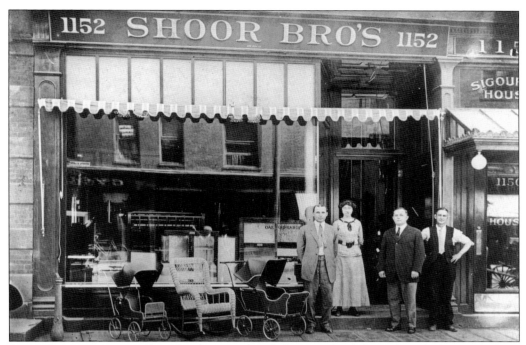

SHOOR BROTHERS, 1908. Shoor Brothers was founded in 1908 by Philip and Jacob Shoor. Abraham Shoor joined the company after Philip left. It was originally located in the Sigourney House (pictured) and later moved to Main Street and then Trumbull Street. At one time, it was the leading furniture store in Hartford. In 1928, it was bought by the Reliable Stores Corporation.

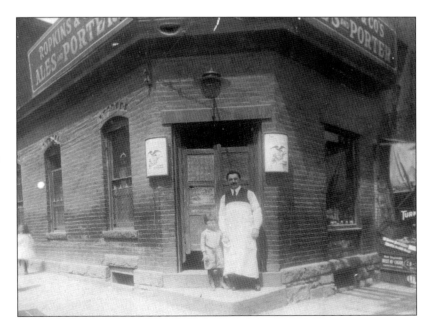

YELLIN'S SALOON, c. 1910. Yellin's Saloon was located at 177 Windsor Street in Hartford. Pictured here are proprietor Mayer Yellin and his son Norman, who later became a judge.

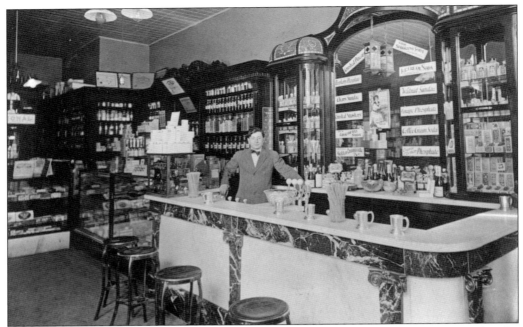

NELSON'S DRUG STORE, C. 1910. Sam Nelson (pictured) was born in Russia in 1884. When he came to Hartford, he worked for Dr. Cantaro, a Russian pharmacist. Although he was hired to do general work, Nelson was able to pass the state Board of Pharmacists exam and later opened his own drugstore on Park Street.

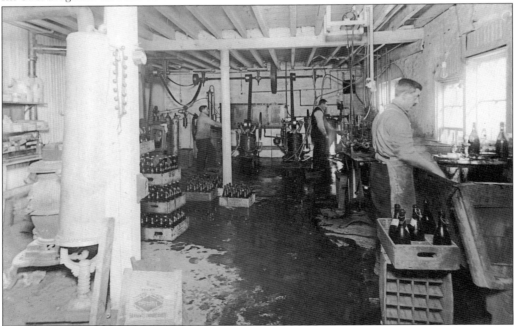

RABINOVITZ SODA BOTTLING, 1914. Samuel Rabinovitz was born in Russia but lived most of his life in Hartford and West Hartford. His soda bottling plant was on Governor Street in Hartford, but he also ran a wholesale tobacco and confectionary business. Mr. Levy, his partner, is at front right.

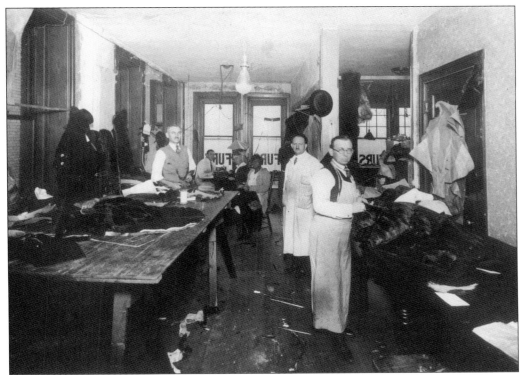

S. MAX & CO. FURRIERS, 1917. Max Sklarinsky (S. Max) and his wife, Rose, came to the United States from Vilna around 1900. He originally worked as a tailor for Sage Allen. In 1912, he founded S. Max & Co. Furriers on Church Street in Hartford. Max also served as president of the Furriers Guild of Hartford.

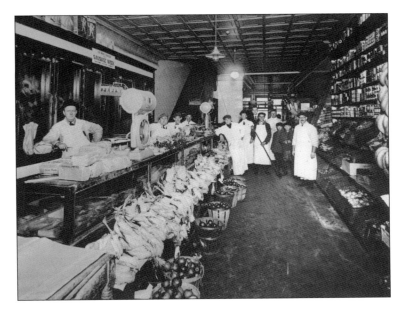

J. KASHMAN & SON'S SPECIALTY MARKET, LATE 1920S. J. Kashman & Sons was a kosher meat market that was founded by Joseph Kashman, a German immigrant who was in the livestock business. It was located on Mulberry Street. His sons also went into the business, and by the 1940s, Seymour Kashman (far right) was the president of the company.

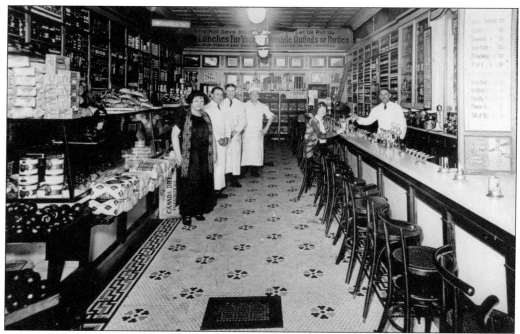

EMPIRE CITY DELICATESSEN AND RESTAURANT, C. 1925. From left to right are Yetta Schwartz (cashier and bookkeeper), Ely Scoler (owner), Nat Burness (sandwich maker), an unidentified chef, and Abe Portner (fountain). The delicatessen was located on Main Street in Hartford. Scoler founded three delicatessen/restaurants. He also owned Scolers on Farmington Avenue, a popular Hartford eatery that later moved to the Bishops Corner area of West Hartford.

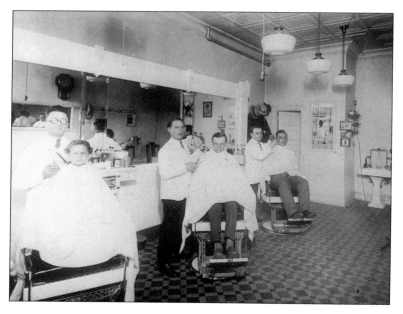

CRYSTAL BARBER SHOP, C. 1925. Jack Molans (left) was the owner of the shop on Albany Avenue for over 25 years. He was born in Russia and immigrated to the United States at a young age. Molans served in the Navy during World War I. He was a member of the Jewish War Veterans, as well as an officer of the Master Barber's Association.

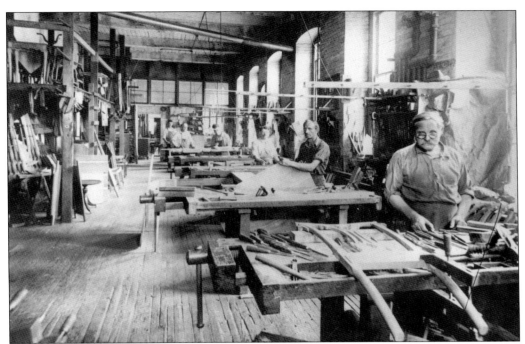

THE NATHAN MARGOLIS SHOP, 1920
(ABOVE) AND A MARGOLIS CHAIR, C. 1920S
(RIGHT). Nathan Margolis was a Lithuanian
refugee who arrived in America with his
family in 1892. He and his father ran an
antiques business in Hartford for five years.
He began making reproduction furniture in
1894 when he opened the Nathan Margolis
Shop on Albany Avenue. His son Harold
took over the business, then known as the
Margolis Shop, until it closed in the mid-
1970s. They also restored antique furniture,
including pieces for Connecticut's Old
State House. Margolis furniture is still
highly prized and valued as antiques in
their own right. The shop's records and
patterns are now at the Henry Francis
DuPont Museum in Winterthur, Delaware.

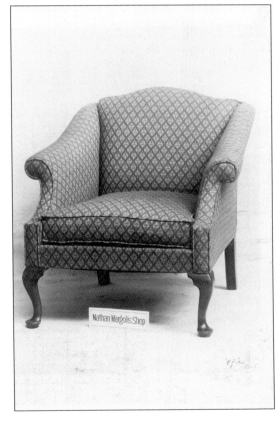

Nathan Margolis Shop

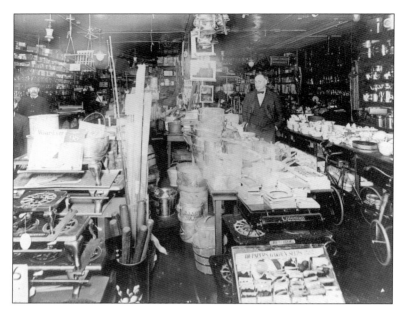

EPSTEIN'S CROCKERY AND HARDWARE, C. 1917. This store was on Front Street in Hartford and sold household items including cookware, appliances, and hardware. In 1922, owner Morris Epstein (right) and several other local businessmen were summoned to court for violating the Connecticut law regarding Sunday sales, which were prohibited at the time.

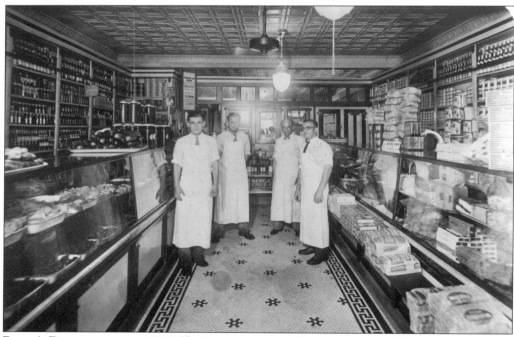

PLATT'S DELICATESSEN, C. 1926. Platt's was a very popular restaurant on Albany Avenue. When one of the original owners left the business in the 1940s, Jack Kalmis, a Russian deli worker from New York, heard about the opening and moved to Hartford to become co-owner. He continued in that position for about 35 years. The deli was also owned by Harry Geri.

ABRAHAM TORCHINSKY'S GROCERY STORE, 1930s. Abraham Torchinsky, along with his father, owned the grocery store that was originally located on Franklin Avenue in Hartford's South End. It later moved to Babcock Street and then New Britain Avenue, where this picture was taken.

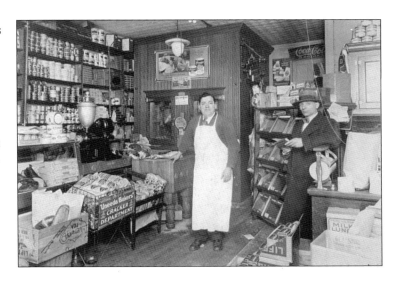

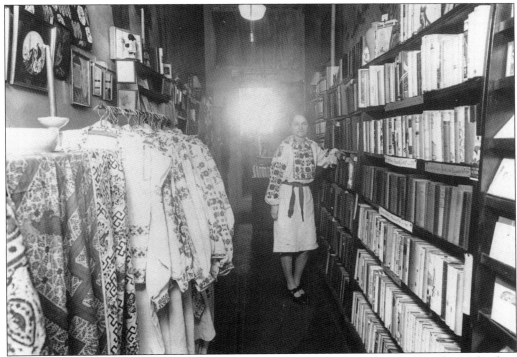

ALADDIN SHOP, C. 1930. Emma Perlstein Cohen was the proprietor of the Aladdin Shop. The shop sold books, cards, and gifts and was located in the Allyn Building on Trumbull Street in Hartford. Emma married Dr. Morris Cohen, and both were active members of many local Jewish organizations. She was a founding member of the Jewish Historical Society and its first president.

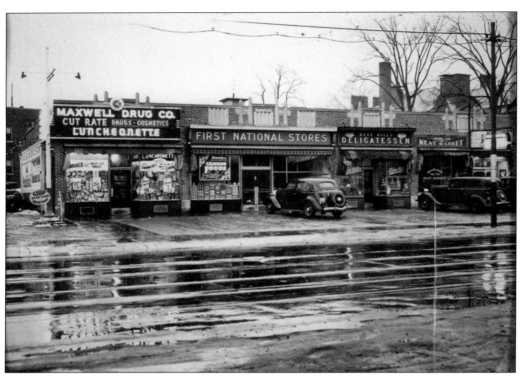

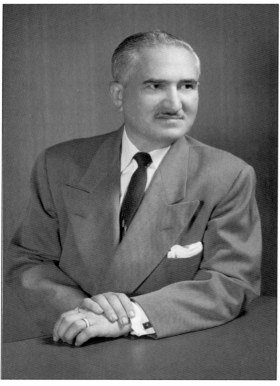

MAXWELL DRUG CO., C. 1920S (ABOVE) AND MAXWELL RULNICK C. 1955 (LEFT). Maxwell Rulnick (1905–1960), a Russian immigrant, opened Maxwell's Drug Company in 1936, and it soon became an institution on Albany Avenue. He eventually owned six drugstores, with locations in East Hartford, West Hartford, Hamden, and Torrington. Maxwell began working in the pharmacy business in 1919 while still in grammar school and obtained his pharmacist's license in 1923. In 1947, he was joined by his brother Morris. Maxwell was an innovator, whose stores were among the first to install air conditioning and have a lunch counter, which provided not only soft drinks, but also meals. His stores were popular gathering places for both adults and teens. (Left, courtesy of the Rulnick family.)

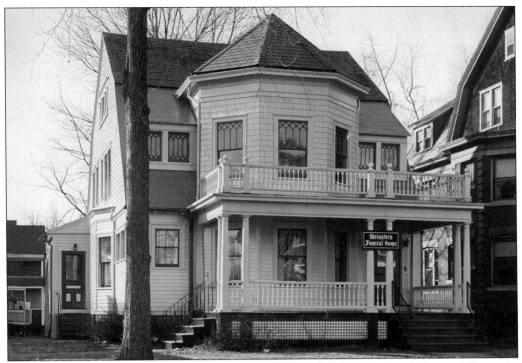

WEINSTEIN'S MORTUARY, 1940. Weinstein's was started by brothers Paul and Herman Weinstein on Albany Avenue in 1940. Herman was the first licensed Jewish funeral director in Hartford. Weinstein's Mortuary moved to Farmington Avenue in 1950 and had the first building in the area constructed specifically for mortuary and funeral services. It continues to be a family-run business today. (Courtesy of Morton Weinstein.)

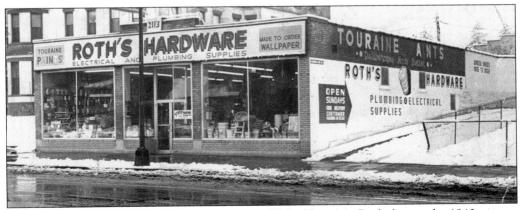

ROTH'S HARDWARE, C. 1950. The store was established by a Mr. Roth, but in the 1940s, it was purchased by Simon Rosenthal and his brother. It was later sold to Rosenthal's son-in-law Joe Fichandler. The store moved from its original location on Windsor Street to Main Street in the 1960s after a fire destroyed the building.

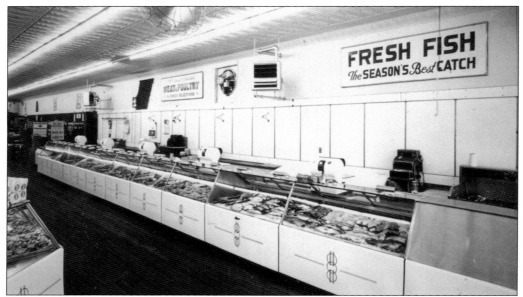

CROWN MARKET, C. 1950. Sam Smith, Samuel Sowalsky, and Meyer Goldfield founded the Crown Kosher Supermarket on Albany Avenue in 1940, and Jack Sloat bought out Meyer Goldfield a year later. The Crown not only sold kosher packaged products but also *kashered* meat and poultry. It remains a community institution today, relocating from Hartford to West Hartford in 1967 as more Jews moved to the suburbs.

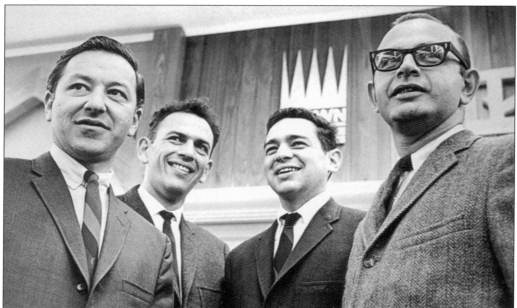

OWNERS OF CROWN MARKET, 1967. From left to right are Ralph Seltzer, Marvin Kramer, William Sloat, and Allan Smith. The store started as a group of concessions within the building. The owners ran the meat and delicatessen departments, while others operated the bakery, produce section, and various departments. This changed with the move to West Hartford, when all of these sections consolidated and were run by the Crown.

ROBBINS DELICATESSEN
AND RESTAURANT, 1958.
Robbins Delicatessen
was founded by Harry
Robbins. It was originally
located on Windsor
Street. In the 1930s, it
moved across the street
from the State Theater,
where it was frequented
by theater and vaudeville
performers, including
Jimmy Durante and Eddie
Cantor. This photograph
shows its Main Street
location, where it moved
in 1950. It closed in
1961. (Photograph by
the *Hartford Courant*.)

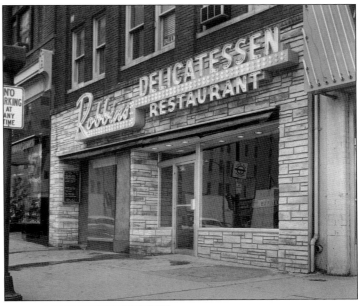

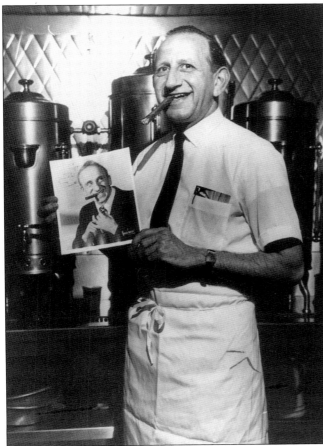

PHILIP "SPEEDY" COHN,
1960. Philip, or Phil, Cohn
(1912–1996) worked at Robbins
Delicatessen for 32 years, until
it closed in the 1960s. He got
his nickname for his fast service
and quick wit. He served, and
came to know, many of the
vaudeville stars who appeared
at the State Theater nearby.
After the restaurant was
demolished, Cohn volunteered
at the Bloomfield Senior Center
for many years. (Photograph
by the *Hartford Courant*.)

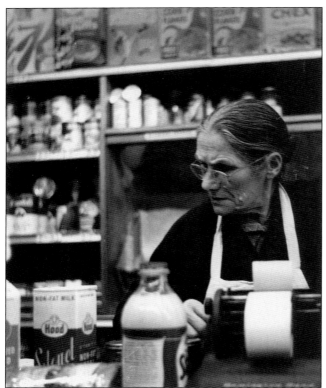

FRUCHTMAN'S DELICATESSEN, c. 1940. Fannie Fruchtman emigrated from Poland to the United States when she was 14. She worked in Manhattan for a number of years and moved to Hartford after her husband's death. She opened Fruchtman's Delicatessen in 1929. It was a well-known neighborhood business on Albany Avenue until she retired in 1970.

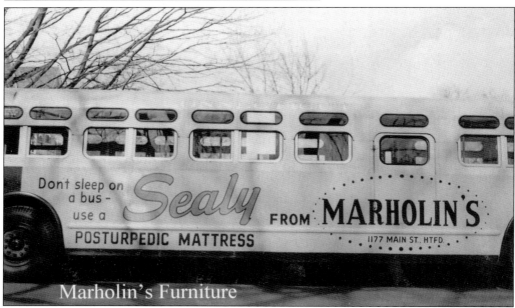

MARHOLIN'S, c. 1960s. David Marholin started this business in 1909 as a bicycle shop. In 1932, furniture was introduced to the store. After David's death in 1946, his widow, Marguerita, and sons Arnold and William took over the store on Main Street. In 1965, they absorbed Lane Furniture. The store was sold in 1984.

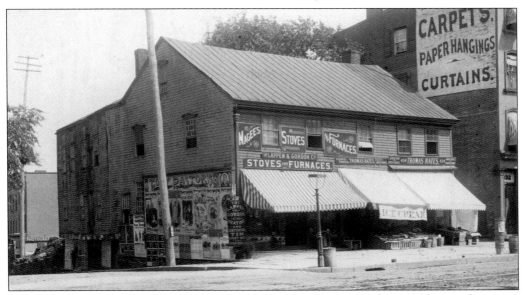

LAPPEN FURNITURE, 1892. The store was founded by Harry Lappen and opened first on the corner of Talcott and Main Streets, selling stoves and furnaces. The business moved to the south end of Main Street around 1906 and became one of the largest fireplace equipment establishments in New England. By 1942, it was co-owned by Harry and his son Seymour. (Courtesy of the Hartford History Center, Hartford Public Library.)

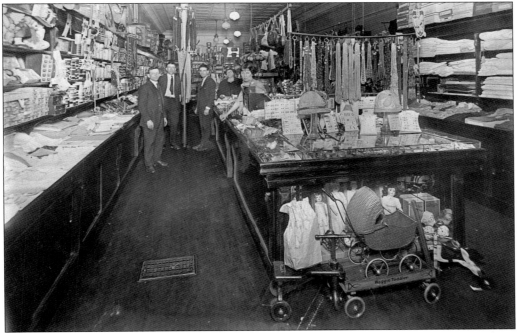

KAMINS 5 & 10, 1918. Aaron Kamins opened Kamins on Main Street around 1918. He was later joined by his brother-in-law William Parks. After Aaron's death in 1937, his wife, Ann, and son Morris helped run the business. Their move to Albany Avenue was very welcome because of the store's enormous inventory. Suburban branches opened in the late 1950s.

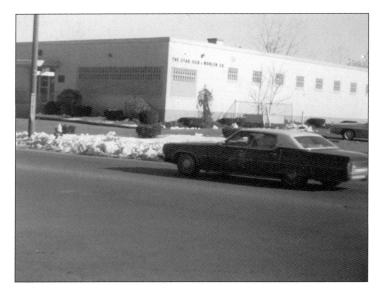

STAR SILK & WOOLEN CO., 1960s. This company on Windsor Street was founded in 1918 by Bennie Novarr and David Freedman. After arriving in Hartford, Novarr worked for Freedman at a dry goods store, and then they became partners in Star Silk & Woolen, a successful wholesale distributor of sheets, pillowcases, blankets, and silk and woolen goods. In 1964, they moved into a new facility on Market Street.

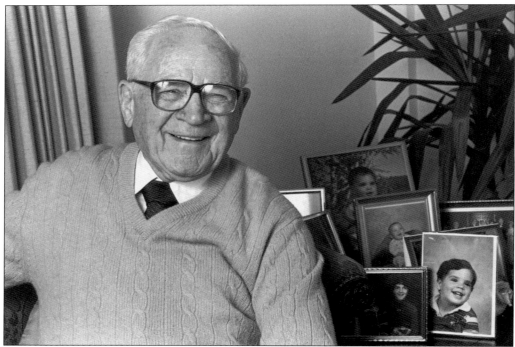

BENNIE NOVARR, C. 1984. Bennie Novarr (1889–1993) was born in Russia and came to the United States in 1913. Star Silk & Woolen, which he opened with his partner, David Freedman, became a very successful wholesale dry goods distributor. Eventually, Novarr's son Leo and son-in-law Mel Katzman ran the business, followed by their sons. Bennie worked at the store until he was 99.

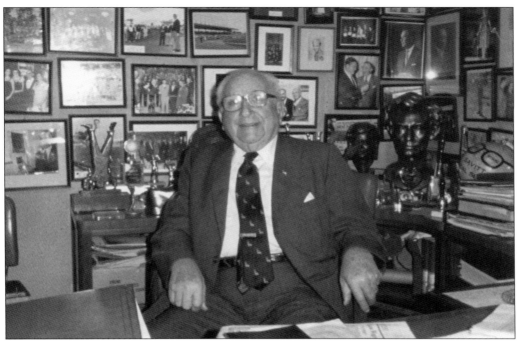

WILLIAM "BILL" SAVITT, 1986. Bill Savitt (1901–1995) founded Savitt Jewelers in 1919 on Park Street. The business moved to 35 Asylum Street, where he advertised as being only "35 seconds from Main Street." His slogan "P.O.M.G." (peace of mind guaranteed) became well known in the community. Savitt was also a philanthropist. He retired in 1986 after 68 years in business. (Courtesy of the Hartford History Center, Hartford Public Library.)

MAYRON'S BAKERY, 1961. Mayron's, owned by Martin Levine and Mayron Keizerstein, was a popular bakery on Albany Avenue, known for its rye bread and Kaiser rolls. For President Kennedy's birthday, Democratic Connecticut congressman Emilio Daddario arranged for Mayron's to create a 30-layer, five-foot-high cake with a sugar replica of the White House. It was delivered to Washington by armored car. (Courtesy of the John F. Kennedy Presidential Library.)

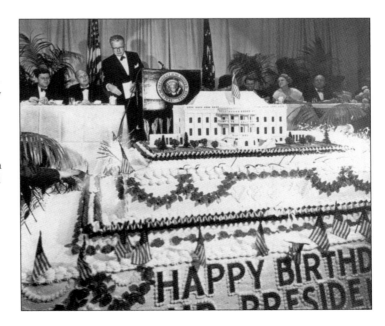

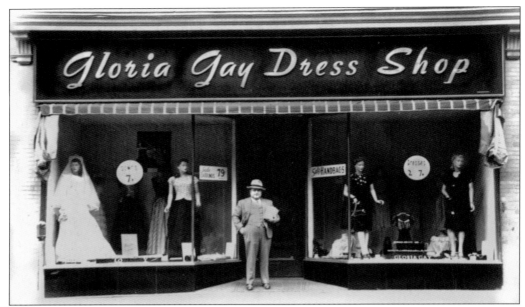

GLORIA GAY DRESS SHOP, 1947. Located at 18 Church Street, the shop was opened in 1947 by Nathan Myerson and his wife, Tania, a Russian immigrant. They made custom wedding gowns and bridal attire. The shop was part of a group of stores that decided to keep later hours to promote downtown as a shopping destination.

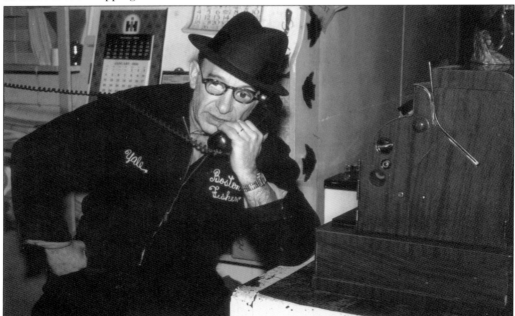

YALE COHN, 1973. Opened in 1933 by Yale Cohn (1908–1995), the Bostonian Fishery operated for over 60 years on Park Street in Hartford. Cohn ran the business until his retirement in 1993, assisted by his son-in-law Mark Gordon, who took over the business with his wife, Barbara, after Cohn's retirement. The business moved to Bloomfield in 1994 and closed in 1999. (Courtesy of Barbara Gordon.)

SHERROW TEXTILES, 1962.
Owners Miriam and Sam
Sherrow opened the shop
in 1939 on Main Street but
moved to a larger location
on Main Street in the mid-
1940s. They specialized
in curtains, bedding,
and fabrics for interior
decorating. After Sam's
death in 1953, Miriam
took over the business
until it was later sold.

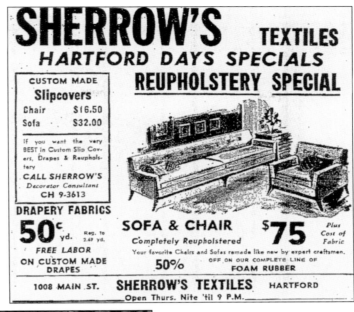

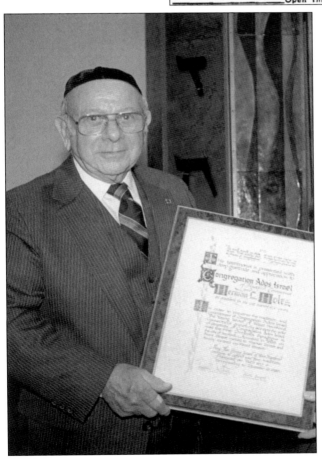

HERMAN HOLTZ, C. 1980S.
Inspired by his work with Jewish
soldiers killed in battle during
World War II, Herman Holtz
(1901–1990) created the Hebrew
Funeral Association after his
return from the war in 1945, to
formalize Hartford's burial society,
Chesed Shel Emes. Today, it
remains a family-run business.
(Courtesy of Leonard Holtz.)

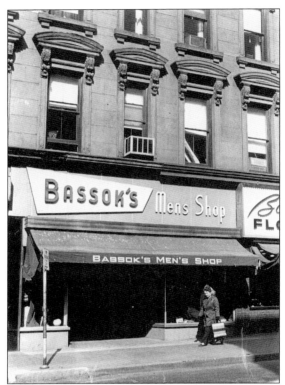

BASSOK'S CLOTHING STORE, C. 1960S. Benjamin "Bennie" Bassok (d. 1983) immigrated to Hartford from Russia in 1922. He opened his store on Front Street in 1930, selling stylish high-quality men's clothing. He remained there through two floods and a hurricane, until the construction of the Founders Bridge forced him to move temporarily to Main Street in 1957. By the mid-1960s, Bassok's had relocated to Asylum Street.

MANDELL BROTHERS WOODLAND SERVICE STATION, C. 1950S. This legendary neighborhood Texaco gas station was owned by the Mandell brothers Max ("Nosh"), Louis ("Lobs") and Morris ("Jiggs"). It was located on the corner of Harrison Place and Woodland Street. The station provided personal, hands-on service from 1946 to 1983. (Courtesy of Laurie Mandell.)

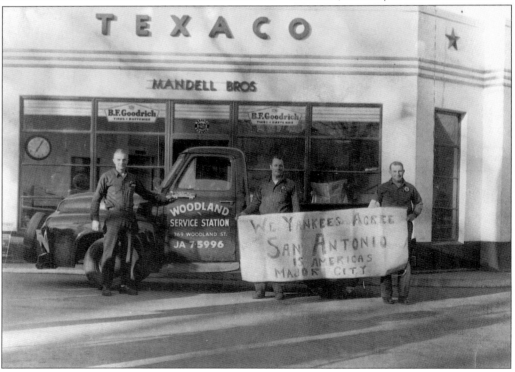

Two

RELIGIOUS LIFE

In the early years of the state, the Congregational Church retained a strong hold on Connecticut and was tax supported. In 1818, a constitutional convention voted to disestablish the church, but public worship by Jews was not allowed until 1843. In that year, two groups—one in Hartford and one in New Haven—petitioned to have the same rights as Christians. The Hartford congregation, Beth Israel, began its life as a German Orthodox synagogue. In 1876, they erected the first building in Connecticut specifically designed to be a synagogue. In 1878, this congregation chose to join the Reform movement.

As more Eastern European Jews moved to the area, new Orthodox synagogues were founded and most flourished. In 1919, a group of Orthodox immigrants met to form a Conservative congregation called B'nai Israel. It quickly changed its name to The Emanuel Synagogue, and after officially joining the Conservative movement, it hired its first rabbi, Abraham Nowak. Other Conservative and Reform synagogues followed. As people moved away from the East Side, new buildings were erected or purchased in the North End. Over time, many synagogues left the city and followed their congregants to the suburbs. A number also merged to form new entities. Today, there are no active synagogues located in Hartford, although a number of these buildings have been repurposed as churches or community facilities and still retain some of the original Jewish religious ornamentation.

Hartford has been fortunate to have many notable religious leaders who were also prominent on the national stage. Rabbi Morris Silverman of The Emanuel Synagogue compiled, translated, and edited prayer books for adults and children that became standard in the Conservative movement. It was also one of the first congregations to allow women to have a Friday night Bat Mitzvah. Rabbi Abraham AvRutick of Agudas Achim was a well-known leader in the Orthodox movement and Rabbi Abraham Feldman of Congregation Beth Israel was the editor of the *Jewish Ledger* and a well-known figure in the community, particularly on interfaith issues.

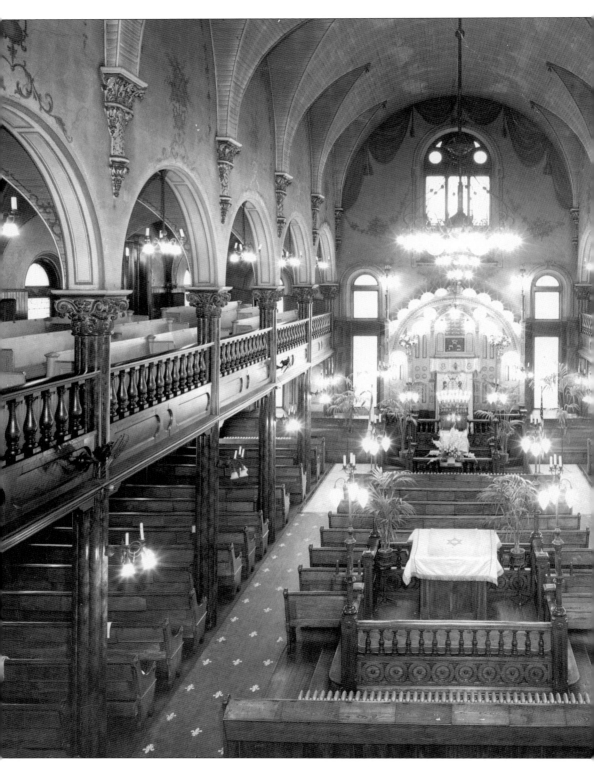

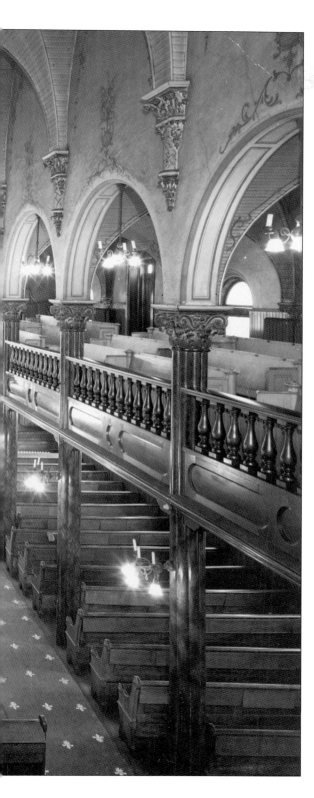

ADOS ISRAEL, MARKET STREET, INTERIOR, c. 1940s. The congregation of Ados Israel was originally organized as the Association of Brothers, Children of Israel. It was founded by Nathan Kempner (1884–1909), the first president, who served for 25 years. Beginning in 1872, the congregants met in private homes and then bought a lot on Market Street. Construction began in 1898, and the synagogue was dedicated in 1899, with a great deal of pomp and ceremony, including an appearance by Gov. Morgan Bulkeley. At the time of its construction, it was considered the most imposing synagogue building in New England, with sanctuary seating for 1,000. The synagogue provided an Orthodox place of worship for new immigrants after Congregation Beth Israel joined the Reform movement.

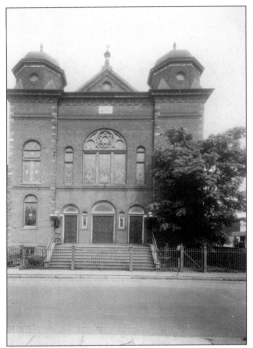

ADOS ISRAEL, MARKET STREET, EXTERIOR, c. 1940S (LEFT) AND FLOOD, 1936 (BELOW). In 1936, the Connecticut River overflowed and flooded the streets of Hartford. As the water rose, members of Ados Israel became concerned about the safety of the Torah scrolls that were still inside the building. One member of the congregation, Herman L. Holtz, took a police boat to the synagogue to save them (pictured below). The synagogue suffered significant damage from the flooding. In 1963, urban renewal and the planned demolition of the building forced the congregation to sell it and move to a new location on Pearl Street. (Below, courtesy of Leonard Holtz.)

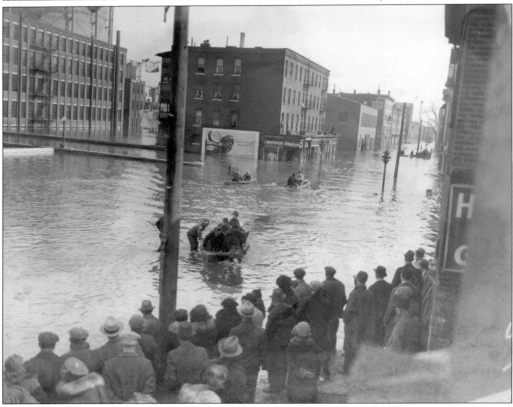

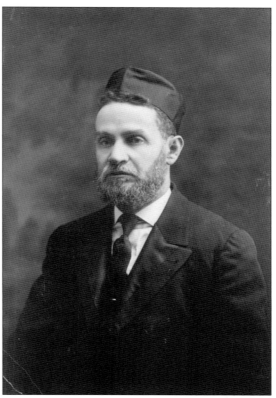

RABBI HUREWITZ, EARLY 1900s (RIGHT) AND THE ADOS ISRAEL CHOIR, C. 1914 (BELOW). Rabbi Isaac Hurewitz (1868–1935) came to Hartford in 1893 and was the first Orthodox rabbi in the city. He was the first spiritual leader of Ados Israel but subsequently also served at Agudas Achim and Beth Hamedrosh Hagodol. A recognized Talmudic scholar, Rabbi Hurewitz was the editor of a Yiddish publication, the *Jewish Voice*. He was also instrumental in establishing many Jewish charitable and educational institutions. This choir was led by conductor Joseph Brown, who came to Hartford in 1900. He served under a number of cantors and taught violin. Many prominent local musicians were among his students.

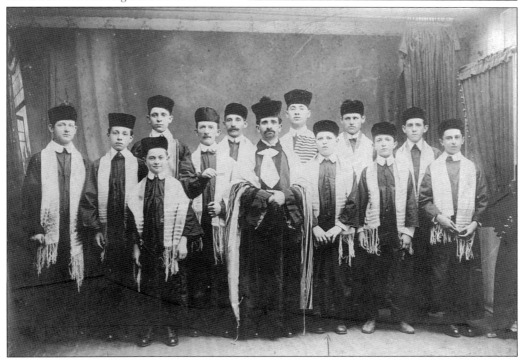

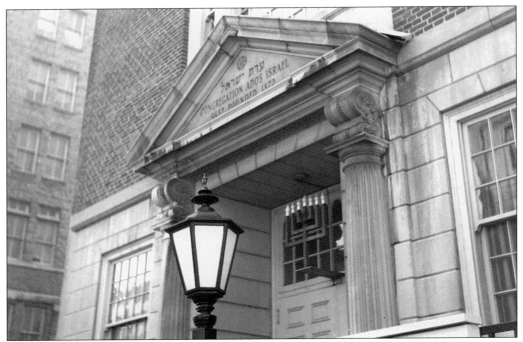

ADOS ISRAEL SYNAGOGUE, PEARL STREET, HARTFORD, 1965. The synagogue relocated to Pearl Street from Market Street. The congregation decided to remain in the city to serve the needs of workers in downtown Hartford. The building, which had been built as a church, did not have a gallery for women. Women sat on one side of a central aisle, and men on the other side. Due to a large population swing to the suburbs, the congregation gradually dwindled until it was no longer feasible to maintain the building and its contents. The last service took place in November 1986. The ark was moved to a newly built synagogue, Congregation Kol Haverim, in Glastonbury, Connecticut.

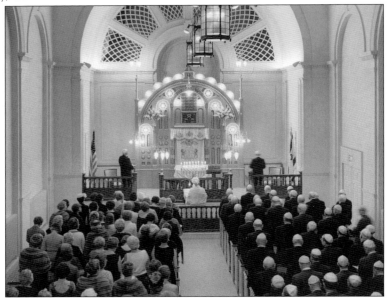

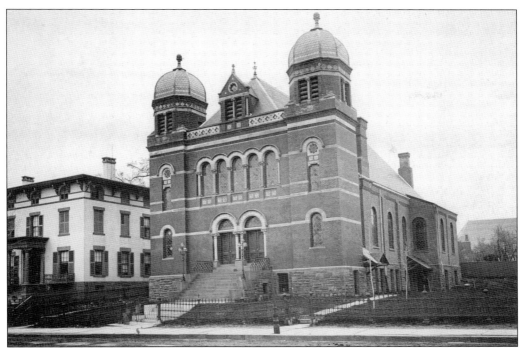

CONGREGATION BETH ISRAEL EXTERIOR, EARLY 1900S (ABOVE) AND CONFIRMATION, 1911 (BELOW).
Beth Israel was established in 1843 when the Connecticut state legislature first allowed public worship for Jews, and is one of the state's oldest congregations. It was originally Orthodox, and most members were German Jews. Initially they gathered in homes, until they bought a church building in 1856 and renamed it Touro Hall. It was used for meetings and services, and space was rented to other organizations. Following a fire in 1875, land was purchased on Charter Oak Avenue. The cornerstone was laid in 1875, and the building was dedicated in 1876. In 1877, the congregation decided to embrace Reform Judaism and was among the founding members of the Union of American Hebrew Congregations (now the Union for Reform Judaism).

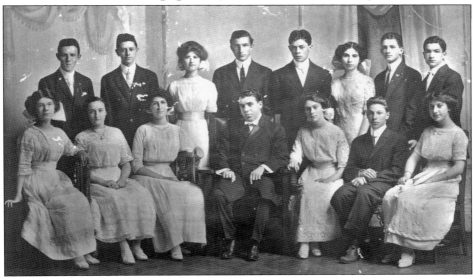

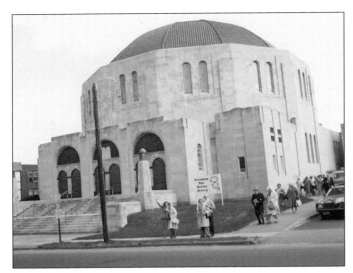

CONGREGATION BETH ISRAEL, FARMINGTON AVENUE, WEST HARTFORD, 1978. In 1936, the congregation moved to their present location on Farmington Avenue in West Hartford. Today, it is one of the largest Reform synagogues in the Northeast. Its building, designed by Charles Greco, is an excellent example of Byzantine architecture. Congregation Beth Israel was the first Hartford congregation to construct a new building in the suburbs, to better serve its relocating members.

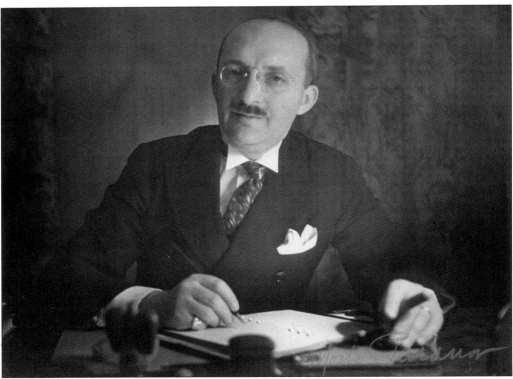

RABBI ABRAHAM FELDMAN, C. 1930S. Rabbi Feldman (1893–1977) came to Congregation Beth Israel in 1925 and became locally prominent and well known as a leader in the Reform movement. He was an ardent Zionist and was active in many interfaith and civil rights organizations. In addition, he was a founder and editor of the *Connecticut Jewish Ledger*. After his retirement in 1968, Rabbi Feldman served Congregation Beth Israel as rabbi emeritus.

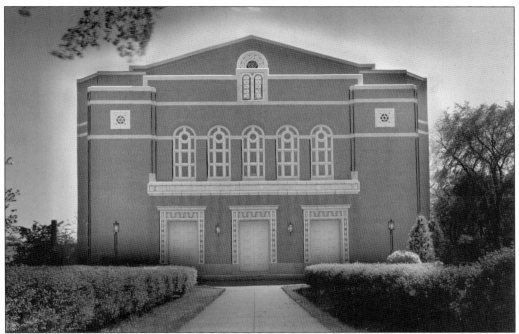

THE EMANUEL SYNAGOGUE, GREENFIELD STREET, 1960S (ABOVE) AND MOHEGAN DRIVE, WEST HARTFORD, 2015 (BELOW). The Emanuel Synagogue was Hartford's first Conservative congregation. Organized in 1919, its original name was B'nai Israel. Their first building was a converted church on Hartford's Main Street. In an unusual move, the congregation advertised in the city directory as a "Jewish Modern Synagogue," and rapid growth soon required more space. In 1924, they built the largest synagogue in the city at that time on Greenfield Street, with a sanctuary that could seat 1,000. In 1956, a new school and auditorium were built in West Hartford to accommodate members who had moved to the suburbs. A few years later, the congregation decided to relocate the entire synagogue to West Hartford. Until 1967, services were held in both locations. The new sanctuary was completed in the early 1970s.

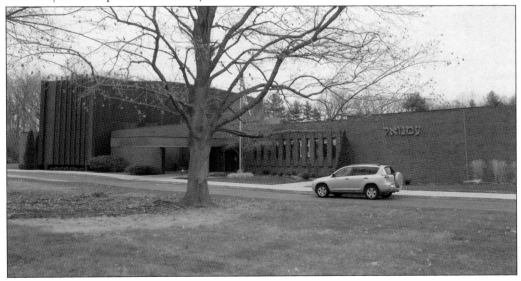

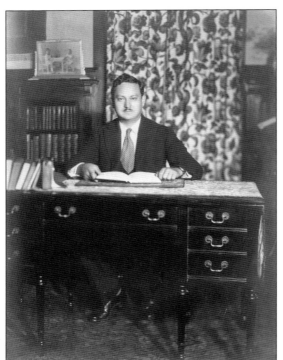

RABBI MORRIS SILVERMAN, C. 1918.
Rabbi Silverman (1894–1972) was
the religious leader of The Emanuel
Synagogue from 1923 to 1961 and a
nationally known Conservative leader.
A prolific writer, he edited 12 prayer
books that were in national use and
contributed to the *Encyclopedia Judaica*.
He also compiled an outstanding
history of his community, *Hartford
Jews, 1659–1970*. Rabbi Silverman
served on the Connecticut Civil
Rights Commission for 22 years.

**CANTOR ARTHUR KORET AT THE
EMANUEL SYNAGOGUE, 1950S.** Cantor
Koret (1916–1990), far right, was
Hartford's first locally born cantor and
served at The Emanuel Synagogue
for 38 years. He produced a number
of recordings and gained a national
reputation. He also served on the
voice faculty at the Hartt School of
Music at the University of Hartford.

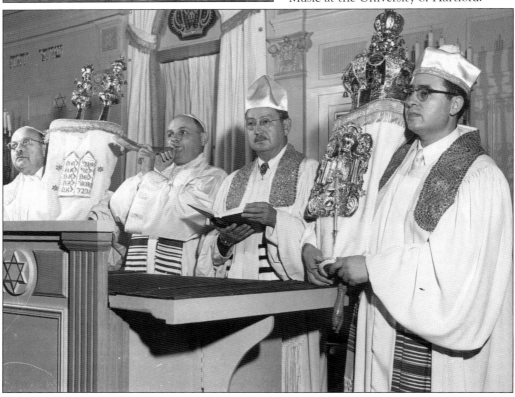

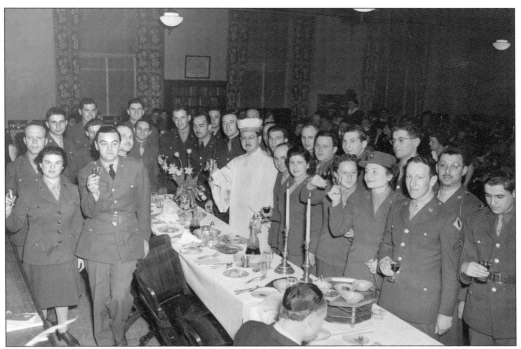

RABBI SILVERMAN AT USO SEDER, 1940s. During World War II, The Emanuel Synagogue hosted a Passover Seder for the USO (United Services Organization), a group that supports men and women in the military. Rabbi Morris Silverman stands in the center of the group.

AGUDAS ACHIM, GREENFIELD STREET, SCHOOL GROUND BREAKING, 1956. At one time, Agudas Achim was the largest Orthodox congregation in Connecticut. Its complete name was Agudas Achim Anshei Sefard, but it was known as the Rumainishe Shul because it was founded by Romanian Jews and followed the Sephardic prayer tradition.

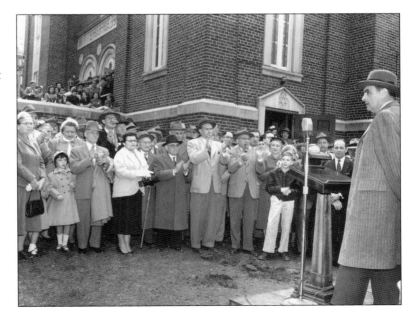

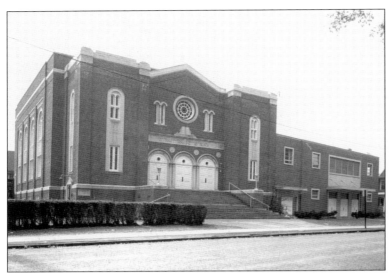

AGUDAS ACHIM, GREENFIELD STREET, EXTERIOR, C. 1960S. The congregation of Agudas Achim incorporated in 1898, and their first building was located on Market Street. They later moved to Greenfield Street and then to North Main Street in West Hartford.

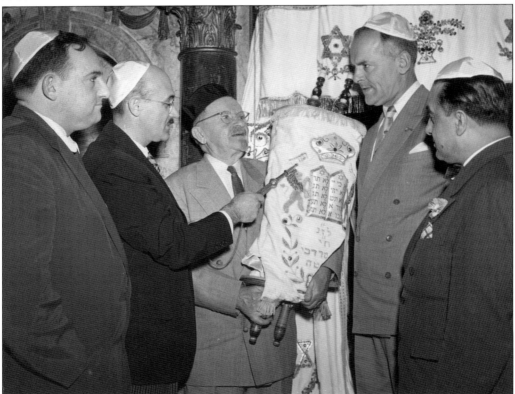

RABBI ABRAHAM AVRUTICK, LATE 1950S. Rabbi AvRutick (1910–1982), second from left, was the religious leader of Agudas Achim from 1946–1982. He became president of the Rabbinical Council of America, the national Orthodox rabbinical group, and was a leading spokesman for Orthodox Judaism. He founded the Va'ad Hakashruth, which supervised the sale of kosher food in Hartford, and organized a highly successful adult education program for Hartford's Orthodox community.

BETH HAMEDRASH HAGODOL, GARDEN STREET, 1969. This congregation of Eastern European Jews was organized in the early 1900s. In 1921, it merged with Shaarey Torah Synagogue, and a new structure on Garden Street in the North End was built in 1923. The congregation was therefore commonly referred to as the Garden Street Synagogue. In 1926, it merged with Ohave Zedeck. This building is in the Romanesque Revival style.

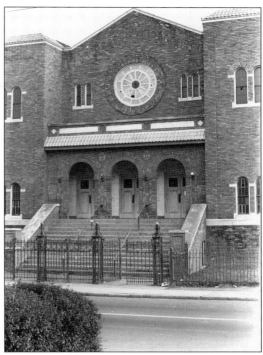

BETH HAMEDRASH HAGODOL ARK, C. 1922. This ark, a large stepped cupboard, was decorated in folk art style with beautifully carved wooden panels. The wall behind the ark is decorated with a mural of the road to heaven and Noah's Ark, and above that is a wheel window with a Star of David in the center. The ark has been restored and is permanently displayed at the JHSGH office.

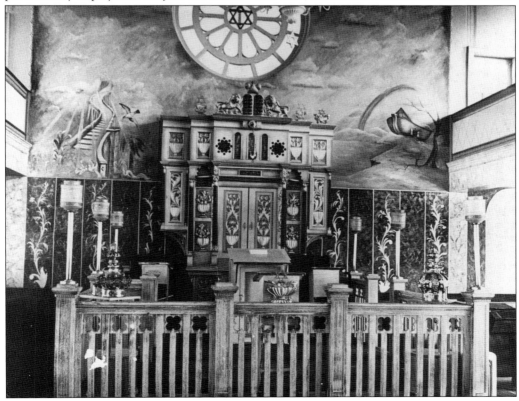

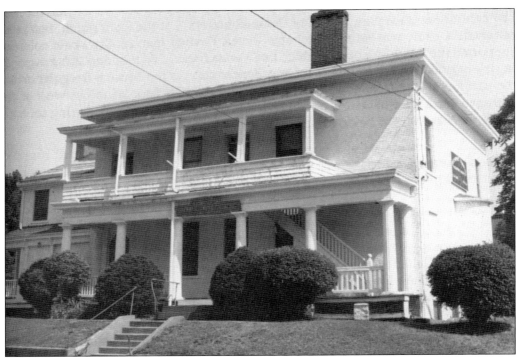

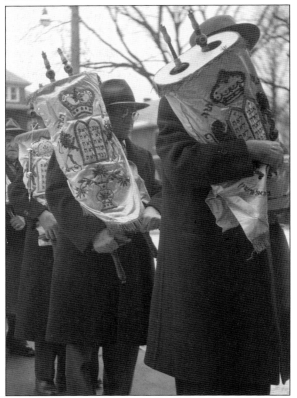

CHEVRE KADISHE TEFERES ISRAEL, MAHL AVENUE, 1980. Chevre Kadishe was organized in 1906 by Russian immigrants. In 1926, it merged with Teferes Israel and moved to Mahl Avenue. In 1956, the congregation built a synagogue on Blue Hills Avenue, known as Teferes Israel, and moved to Brown Street in Bloomfield around 1971.

TRANSPORTING SCROLLS TO TEFERES ISRAEL, 1956. When Teferes Israel built its new synagogue on Blue Hills Avenue, the Torah scrolls were transported to the new building in a special procession. Here, several men bring the scrolls to the new synagogue.

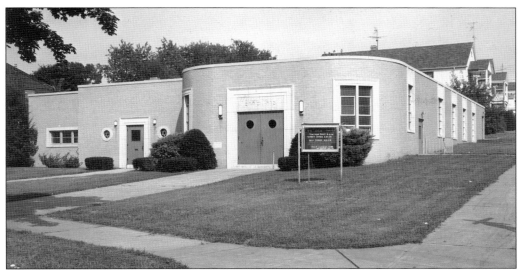

BETH SHOLOM SYNAGOGUE, CORNWALL STREET, 1960S. This Conservative congregation was the result of a 1952 merger of Blue Hills Synagogue and Kahilath Israel Synagogue. In 1955, the congregation broke ground for a new synagogue on Cornwall Street, and the building was constructed in 1957. It did not have enough space for a school, so additional rooms were rented off-site. In 1969, the congregation merged with Beth Hillel Synagogue in Bloomfield.

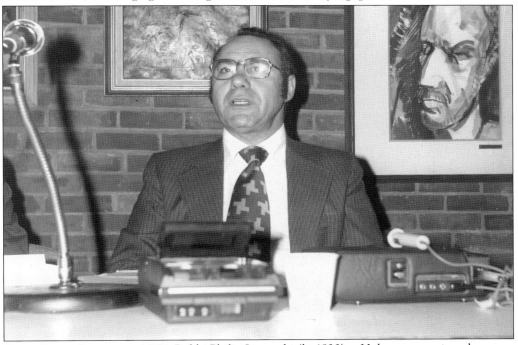

RABBI PHILIP LAZOWSKI, 1977. Rabbi Philip Lazowski (b. 1930), a Holocaust survivor, began as an educator at Beth Sholom Synagogue and was their spiritual leader from 1955–1969. After the merger with Beth Hillel in 1969, he served as rabbi until 2000. He has written 12 books and is rabbi emeritus of The Emanuel Synagogue. He was a chaplain of the Hartford Police Department, the Connecticut state senate, and Hartford Hospital.

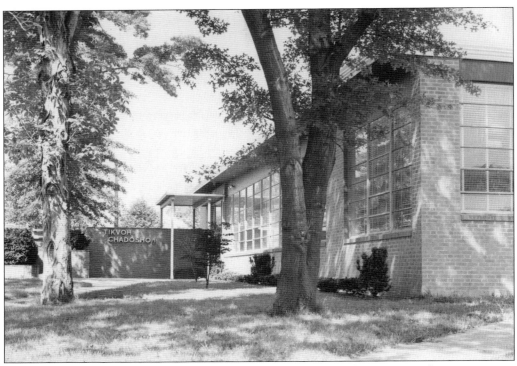

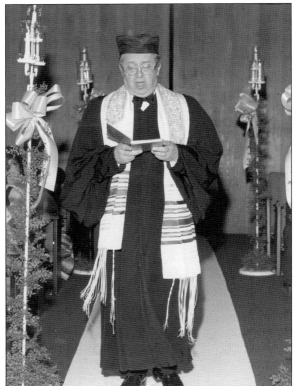

TIKVOH CHADOSHOH, CORNWALL STREET, 1950S. Congregation Tikvoh Chadoshoh was founded in 1942 by a group of German refugees fleeing the Holocaust. The synagogue established its first permanent home in 1957 in Hartford and moved to Blooomfield in 1971. In 2011, it merged with Congregation B'nai Sholom in Newington, to form Congregation B'nai Tikvoh-Sholom.

RABBI HANS BODENHEIMER, 1975. Rabbi Bodenheimer (1913–1999) was born in Germany and entered the rabbinate there. After Kristallnacht in 1938, he was arrested and spent five weeks in the Buchenwald concentration camp before being released. He came to the United States and, with other German immigrants, founded Congregation Tikvoh Chadoshoh (New Hope). He was active in many community organizations and served as chaplain of the Bloomfield Fire Department.

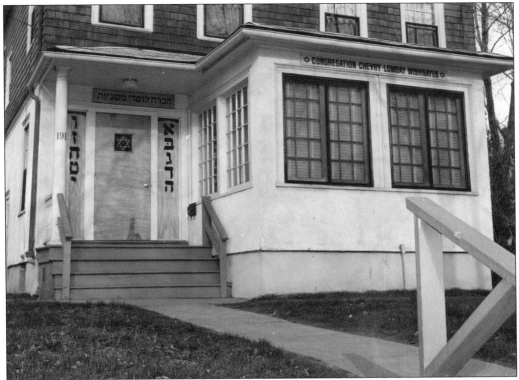

CHEVRY LOMDAY MISHNAYES, WESTBOURNE PARKWAY, 1965. This Orthodox congregation organized by immigrants from Eastern Europe and Russia in 1918 began in an empty store on Windsor Street. A new synagogue was built on Bedford Street in 1927 and moved to Westbourne Parkway in 1965. It was one of the last remaining synagogues in the city after others moved to the suburbs. The congregation disbanded in 1974.

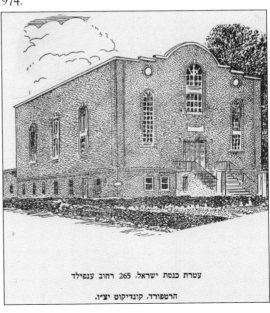

עטרת כנסת ישראל. 265 רחוב ענפילד

הרטפורד. קונדיקוט יצ״ו.

KNESET ISRAEL, ENFIELD STREET, c. 1947. This Orthodox congregation began in 1898 as Congregation Israel of Koretz, because most members came from Koretz, Russia. In 1913, they erected a new building on Suffield Street and remained there until 1946, when they moved to Enfield Street. This was the last synagogue constructed in Hartford. In 1955, they merged with Ateres Israel, and in 1962, they merged again with Beth Hamedrash Hagodol, forming United Synagogues of Greater Hartford.

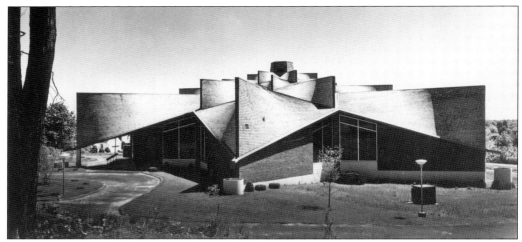

United Synagogues, North Main Street, West Hartford, c. 1960s. In the early 1960s, several small Orthodox synagogues in Hartford faced declining membership and decided to combine, thus forming the United Synagogues of Greater Hartford. They erected a new building on North Main Street in West Hartford in 1967, designed in the shape of a six-pointed Star of David. In 1994, that building was sold, and the congregation moved to Mohawk Drive in West Hartford.

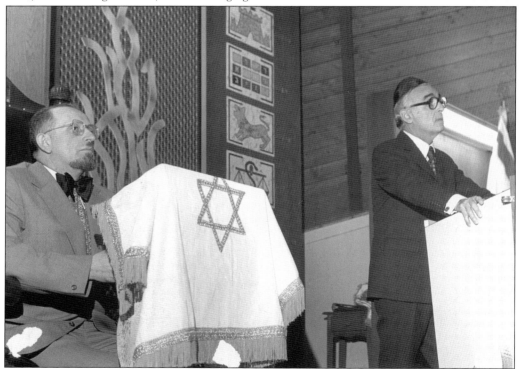

Rabbi Isaac Avigdor, 1967. Rabbi Avigdor (1920–2010), left, was born in Poland, part of a legendary rabbinic family. During the Holocaust, he was a prisoner in the Mathausen concentration camp. He and his family arrived in Hartford in 1955 and he became the rabbi of Ateret Knesseth Israel Synagogue. When it merged with the Garden Street Synagogue to form United Synagogues of Greater Hartford, Rabbi Avigdor served as its spiritual leader for over 30 years.

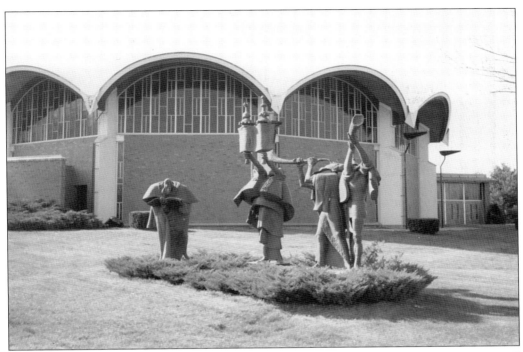

BETH EL TEMPLE OF WEST HARTFORD, ALBANY AVENUE, 1978. By 1953, fifty percent of The Emanuel Synagogue's congregants resided in West Hartford, and the congregation debated whether to relocate or open a branch. One group decided to establish a new synagogue, Beth El Temple. Relations remained cordial, and the congregations shared a Hebrew school. Rabbi Stanley Kessler became their rabbi in 1954, and the new building opened in 1956.

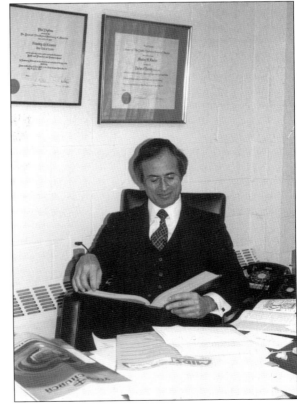

RABBI STANLEY KESSLER, C. 1970S. Rabbi Kessler (b. 1923) arrived in West Hartford in 1954 to lead Beth El Temple and became a nationally known leader in the Conservative movement. As a social activist, Kessler was a Freedom Rider in the 1960s and marched with Dr. Martin Luther King. He has continued to work across religious and racial boundaries to promote tolerance. Rabbi Kessler retired in 1992 and is now rabbi emeritus.

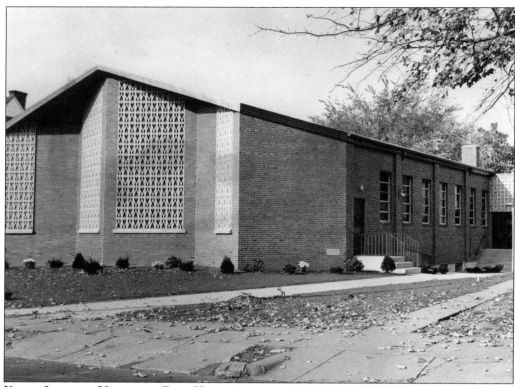

YOUNG ISRAEL OF HARTFORD, BLUE HILLS AVENUE, C. 1962. In 1928, Young Israel was developed as a modern Orthodox congregation. Services were first held at the Agudas Achim. In 1943, the congregation purchased a house on Westbourne Parkway, and in 1962 built this new synagogue on Blue Hills Avenue. In 1969, they moved to Trout Brook Drive in West Hartford.

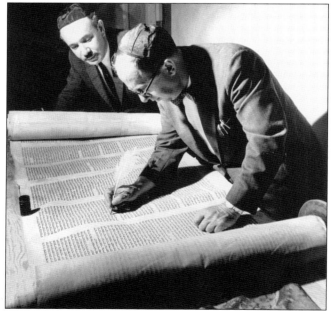

RABBIS HASKEL LINDENTHAL AND HANS BODENHEIMER, C. 1960s. Born in Poland, Rabbi Haskel Lindenthal (1916–2008), left, went to Palestine to study in 1936, where he also served in the Haganah. Losing most of his family in the Holocaust, he immigrated to America. In 1956, he became rabbi at Teferes Israel Synagogue and remained in that position for 40 years, even after its move to Bloomfield. Rabbi Lindenthal also served the community as a *mohel* (ritual Jewish circumciser).

Three

EDUCATION

Jewish education has been an important priority for Hartford's Jews. By 1901, there was a Talmud Torah (religious school) known as the Hebrew Institute. In 1913, it moved to Pleasant Street and became known as the Pleasant Street Talmud Torah. The building in which it was housed also served as a communal center, which sponsored English classes, mutual aid groups, youth groups, and lectures, especially for the newly arrived Eastern European Jews. From 1916 to the late 1920s, it was home to the United Jewish Charities, the Young Men's Hebrew Association (YMHA) and the Young Women's Hebrew Association (YWHA), and a synagogue, Shaarey Torah. As the Jewish community moved to other neighborhoods, enrollment at the Pleasant Street Talmud Torah decreased and it joined other schools to form the United Talmud Torahs of Hartford. As Jews moved further into the suburbs, newly built synagogues developed their own schools, which replaced the community Talmud Torahs. Some parents wanted a more intense Jewish education where religious subjects would be integrated with a general curriculum, and this led to the development of three day schools, two elementary schools, and one high school.

The Yeshiva of Hartford (renamed the Bess and Paul Sigel Hebrew Academy in 1974) was founded as an Orthodox school on Vine Street in 1940. Rapid growth forced a move to the Pleasant Street Hebrew Institute building, then to its own building on Cornwall Street, and, as the Jewish community spread to the suburbs, to Bloomfield. The Solomon Schechter Day School was established in 1971 as the first Conservative school in Connecticut. It first met at The Emanuel Synagogue and then in a renovated West Hartford public school. The Hebrew High School of New England, developed by three communities—Hartford, New Haven, and Springfield, Massachusetts—opened in 1996. It was first housed at Congregation Agudas Achim before moving to its own campus on Bloomfield Avenue in West Hartford.

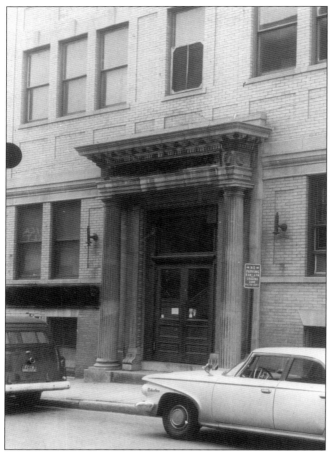

PLEASANT STREET TALMUD TORAH, C. 1950S (LEFT) AND STUDENTS, 1903 (BELOW). In 1901, Orthodox rabbis Isaac S. Hurewitz and Cemach Hoffenberg helped establish the Hartford Hebrew Institute on the city's East Side for after-school Jewish education. In 1902, a house was purchased on Pleasant Street, and the school's role expanded to include assistance for immigrants. It became a community center, with many groups gathering there, including German and Eastern European Jews who united to raise funds to aid oppressed Jews in Europe and to protest the American government's position on limited immigration. It also housed Shaarey Torah Synagogue, United Jewish Charities, the YMHA and YWHA, and Zionist youth groups. Eventually, a larger building on Pleasant Street was purchased. It closed in 1930 as families moved from the area.

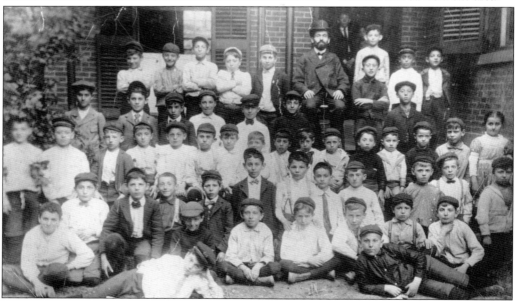

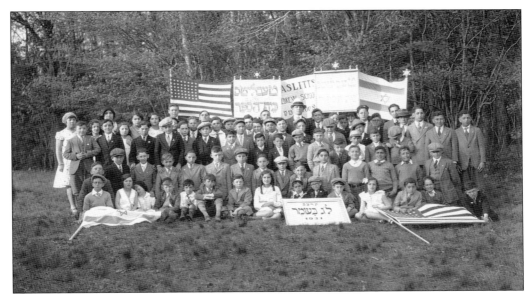

Taslitt's Hebrew School, Lag B'Omer Picnic, 1932. Three classes of students marched to Keney Park in Hartford's North End for this picnic from Taslitt's, a private Hebrew school. Director Eheskel Taslitt preferred to have it called a Beis HaSefer, rather than a Talmud Torah, which was considered a community school.

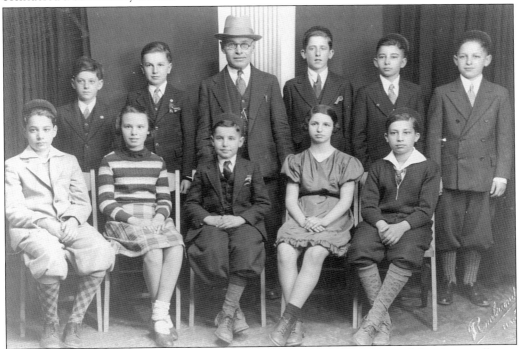

Nelson Street Talmud Torah, 1934. As families moved to different areas of the city, enrollment at the Talmud Torahs decreased. In 1928, the Nelson Street Talmud Torah merged with the Pleasant Street Talmud Torah (also known as the Hebrew Institute). The South End Talmud Torah and the Garden Street Synagogue combined to form the United Talmud Torah.

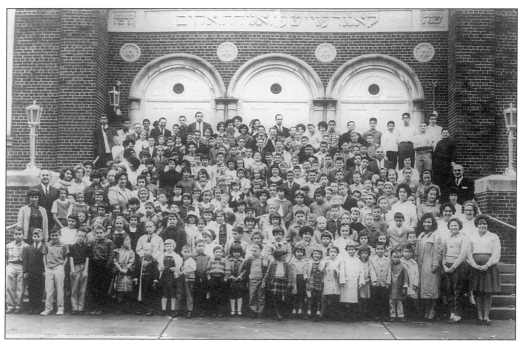

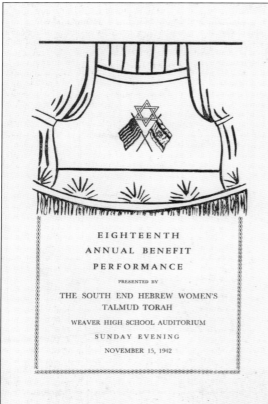

EIGHTEENTH
ANNUAL BENEFIT
PERFORMANCE

PRESENTED BY

THE SOUTH END HEBREW WOMEN'S
TALMUD TORAH

WEAVER HIGH SCHOOL AUDITORIUM

SUNDAY EVENING

NOVEMBER 15, 1942

AGUDAS ACHIM RELIGIOUS SCHOOL STUDENTS, GREENFIELD STREET, C. 1960S. In the early 1950s, with the closing of the local Talmud Torah schools, synagogues began to assume responsibility for educating the children of their members. Agudas Achim added a school wing and auditorium in 1955. For many parents, the quality of the religious school became a compelling reason for joining a particular congregation.

SOUTH END TALMUD TORAH PROGRAM, 1942. A small group of families living in the South End of the city wanted a Hebrew school closer to their homes. An association was formed by a group of women to raise funds, and a building on Congress Street was purchased and remodeled for use as a school and meeting space. Jacob Stein, a well-known Jewish educator, was its first principal.

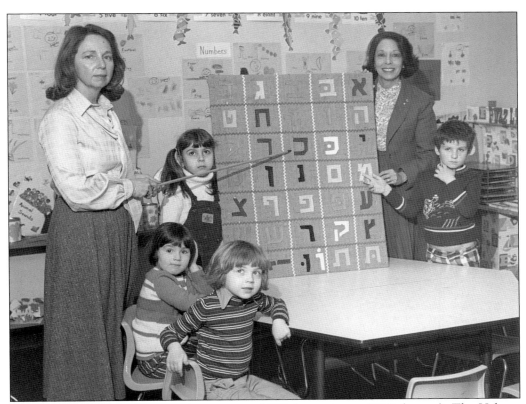

BESS AND PAUL SIGEL HEBREW ACADEMY, C. 1977 (ABOVE) AND 1974 (BELOW). The Hebrew Academy, an Orthodox day school, began as the Hartford Yeshiva in 1940. It was first housed on Vine Street and had seven students. Enrollment doubled by the end of the year, and the school moved to the premises of the Hartford Talmud Torah on Pleasant Street. After nine years at that site, land was purchased on Cornwall Street, and a new building was erected in 1950. The Cornwall Street building expanded in 1962, when increasing enrollment made it necessary to add more classrooms, but in 1965, arsonists set a fire that damaged much of the building. As the Jewish population continued to move to the suburbs, a new building was erected on Gabb Road in Bloomfield in 1974, and the school was renamed for Bess and Paul Sigel.

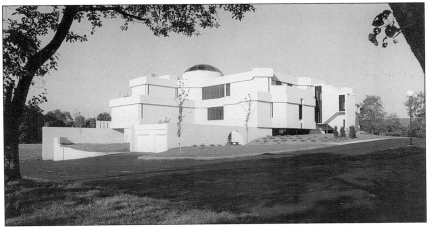

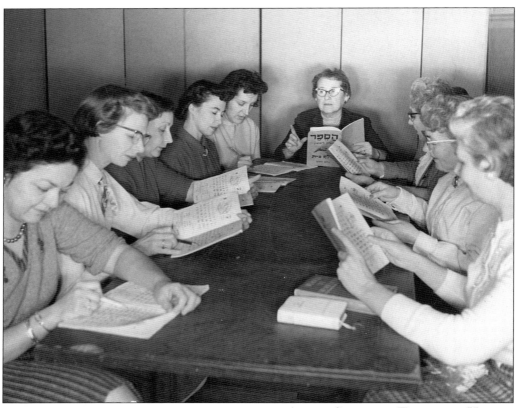

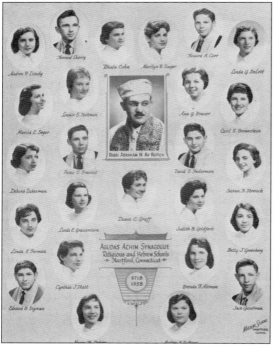

ALTHEA SILVERMAN TEACHING A HEBREW CLASS, 1956. Althea Silverman (1897–1977), wife of Rabbi Morris Silverman, was a Jewish educator and author. She not only taught Hebrew and Bible classes for adults but was also interested in bringing music to children throughout the community. Althea wrote about Jewish history, holidays, and Israel. Among her most popular books were *Habibi and Yow* and *The Jewish Home Beautiful*.

AGUDAS ACHIM RELIGIOUS SCHOOL GRADUATES, 1958. In 1952, four synagogues—Agudas Achim, Beth David, Beth Hamedrash Hagodol, and The Emanuel Synagogue—adopted a mandatory three-days-a-week program for both girls and boys from fourth through seventh grade. Younger children attended a once-a-week program, as did students in grades eight through twelve.

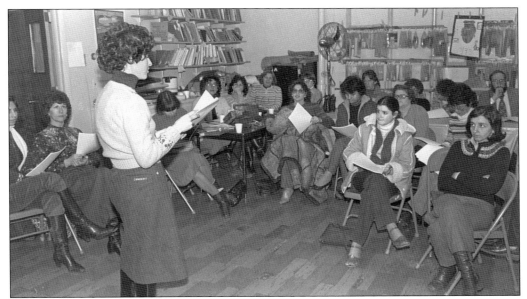

COMMISSION ON JEWISH EDUCATION, C. 1980S. In 1970, the Jewish Federation established the Commission on Jewish Education as a semiautonomous committee to advocate for Jewish education, with Dr. Alfred Weisel as the executive director and its own board of directors. Through the HaMerkaz Educator Resource Center, it offered professional development classes for teachers, school consultations, and other programs. It is now the Commission on Jewish Education and Leadership.

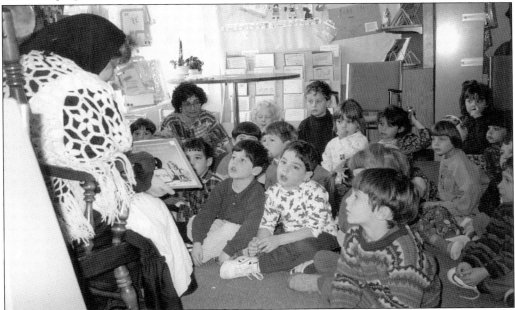

KOOPMAN LIBRARY STORY TIME, 1995. In 1990, Georgette Koopman donated funding for the Koopman Library in the new addition at the Jewish Community Center. It was run by the Jewish Federation's Commission on Jewish Education and contained both the HaMerkaz Educator Resource Center and a Judaic community library, containing fiction and nonfiction for all ages, along with Jewish-themed CDs and films. The library closed in 2014.

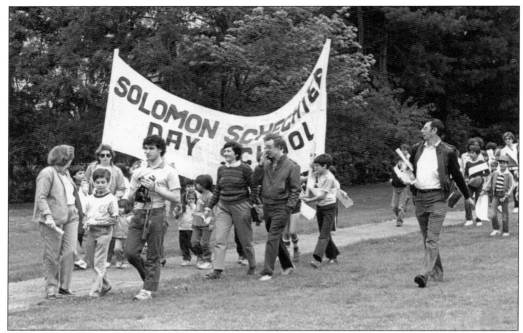

SOLOMON SCHECHTER DAY SCHOOL EVENTS, 1985 (ABOVE) AND 1991 (BELOW). West Hartford's Solomon Schechter Day School, the first Conservative day school in Connecticut, was established in 1971 at The Emanuel Synagogue. Numerous lay leaders and prominent Conservative rabbis were instrumental in this process, along with Rabbi Abraham Feldman, the retired rabbi of the Reform synagogue Congregation Beth Israel. Solomon Schechter, now located on a campus on Buena Vista Road in West Hartford, provides an integrated Judaic and general studies curriculum for children from pre-kindergarten through eighth grade.

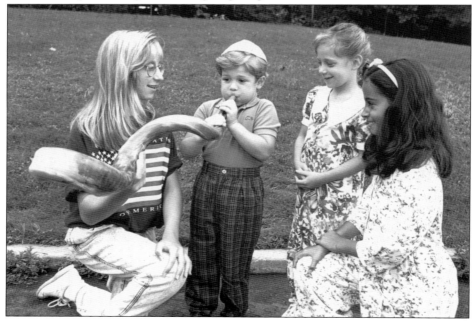

MIDRASHA GRADUATION AT BETH EL TEMPLE, 1973. Midrasha was an after-school joint Conservative high school that began in 1963 with 25 eighth graders and then added one grade each year until it became a four-year program. Eventually, it evolved into a community high school, with students from the Orthodox and Reform communities also attending. This photograph was taken at Beth El Temple, one of the school's sites.

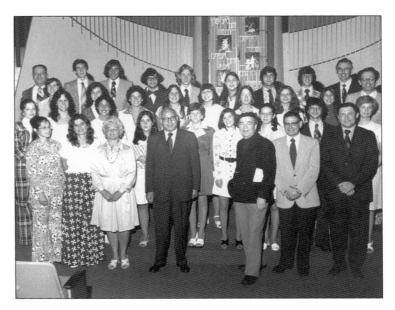

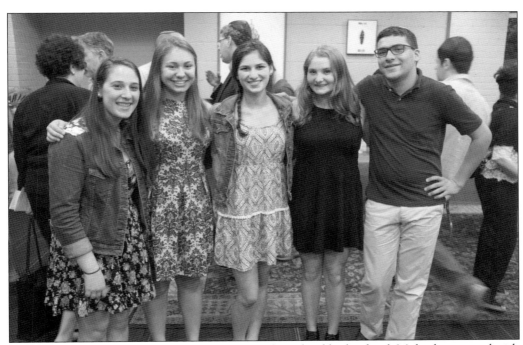

JTCONNECT, 2010s. In 1995, the Conservative after-school high school, Midrasha, merged with Beit Noar, the Reform high school, to form a joint educational program called Yachad. There was strong congregational support across the community, and at its height, the program had 330 students and 30 rabbis and educators. During the 2012–2013 school year, the school changed its name to JTConnect and introduced a revamped and expanded program. (Courtesy of JTConnect.)

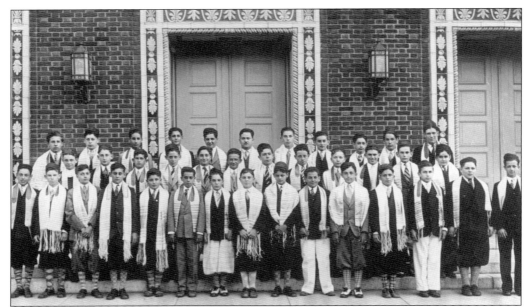

EMANUEL BAR MITZVAH CLUB, 1929. Rabbi Silverman organized the Shabbat morning Bar Mitzvah Club in 1928, and the following year, he instituted a program for post–Bar Mitzvah boys to meet for prayer and breakfast on Sunday mornings. This was in addition to the popular Shabbat morning Junior Congregation services, which attracted several hundred participants each week.

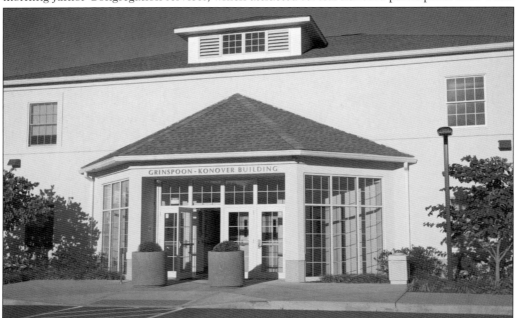

HEBREW HIGH SCHOOL OF NEW ENGLAND, 2015. The school is a modern Orthodox Jewish high school with a dual Judaic and secular curriculum. It was founded in 1996 by members of the Hartford, New Haven, and Springfield, Massachusetts, communities, serving students from throughout New England. The school met at Congregation Agudas Achim until a new campus was built in 2007. (Courtesy of Hebrew High School of New England.)

Four

ZIONISM

Stirred by the writings of Dr. Theodor Herzl, Hartford's Jews were early and strong supporters of Zionism, and many groups for young people and adults were formed. Prominent Zionists from around the world visited Hartford to encourage participation and collect money. After the First Jewish Congress met in Basel, Switzerland, in 1897, a local group organized the B'nai Zion Society. Other organizations soon followed, among them the Zion Guard, the Ladies Zion Society, and the Daughters of Zion. In 1906, the B'nai Zion Society bought a building that soon turned into a center for Zionist activity, hosting clubs for all ages. One of the most active was the Maccabaeans, made up of Hartford High School students, and its girls' auxiliary, the Miriam Zion Society. They held educational meetings and were active fundraisers, especially for the Jewish National Fund, which purchased land in Palestine with donations they collected. Unlike many other communities, Hartford's rabbis of all denominations were ardent Zionists, and they urged their congregants to support Zionism both financially and politically.

In 1914, Henrietta Szold, founder of Hadassah, addressed a small group of local women, who then went on to found the Hartford Chapter of Hadassah. After the signing of the Balfour Declaration in 1917, even more Zionist organizations flourished, and in 1919, the national office of the Zionist Organization of America (ZOA) named Abraham Goldstein of Hartford as state director. He later served as national vice president of the ZOA. On May 23, 1921, Dr. Chaim Weizmann (who later became Israel's first president) and Dr. Albert Einstein came to Hartford. They rode in a motorcade of more than 500 cars, and 15,000 spectators lined the streets. That evening, they raised over $75,000 for Palestine. During World War II, local Zionist leaders traveled to Washington frequently, urging the government to allow Jews greater access to Palestine. In 1948, when Israel was born, there was not only great rejoicing, but also a firm commitment to continue the work necessary for its survival.

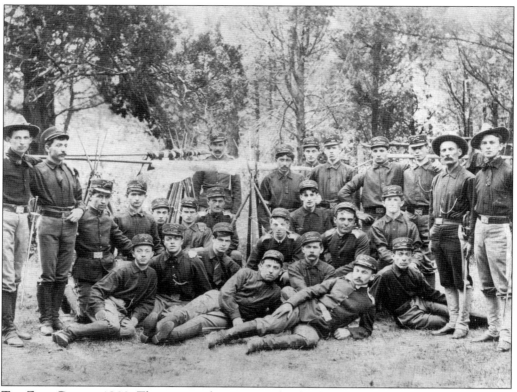

THE ZION GUARD, 1902. This was a military group that held social and athletic events for young people. Members often escorted visiting Jewish dignitaries, including Rabbi Stephen Wise, secretary of the Federation of American Zionists. They also participated in a military escort for Pres. Theodore Roosevelt in 1902. After the Kishinev pogrom in Russia, the group organized a protest meeting and took part in relief efforts for the victims.

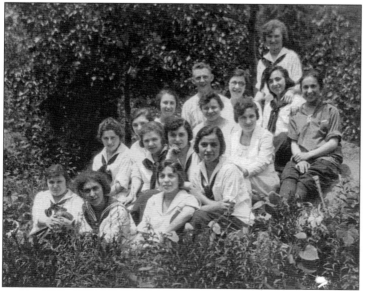

LILIES OF ZION, 1919. This was a chapter of Young Judea, a Zionist youth movement that was founded in 1909 and is the oldest Zionist youth movement in the United States. For years, it operated under the auspices of Hadassah, but became an independent organization in 2012. Today, they sponsor summer camps and college-level programming in Israel.

JEWISH NATIONAL FUND CONVENTION, HARTFORD, 1917. The Jewish National Fund ("Keren Kayemet LeYisrael" in Hebrew) was founded in 1901 to raise funds to purchase property in Palestine from the Ottoman Empire, which controlled the land at that time, and later from the British Mandate. The Jewish National Fund has planted more than 240 million trees, built dams, and helped to develop Tel Aviv.

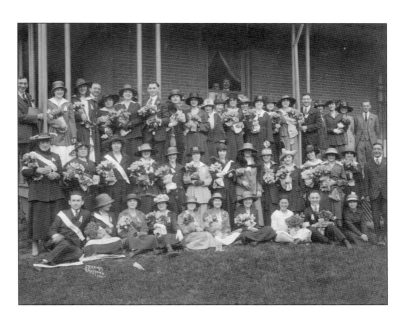

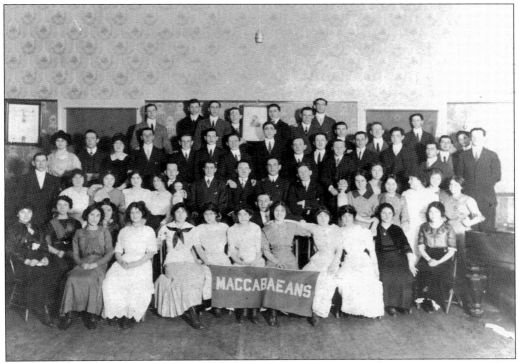

MACCABAEAN ZION CLUB, 1914. This party was held at the Hebrew Institute, to which the members of the Judith Club of Young Judea were invited. The Maccabaean Zion Club was organized in 1907 by students from Hartford High School, and most of them were the children of Eastern European immigrants. Several of their officers later rose to positions of prominence in the community.

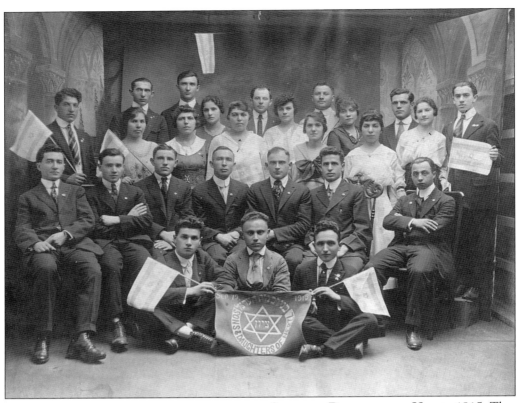

SONS AND DAUGHTERS OF HERZL, 1915. The Sons and Daughters of Herzl was organized around 1915 as a Zionist club for young people. It was a Yiddish speaking group.

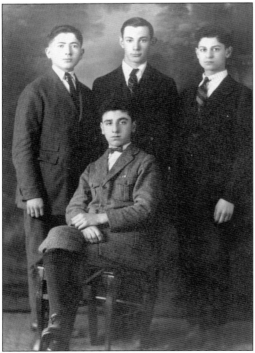

KADIMAH CLUB, 1920S. The Kadimah Club was a Zionist debating society. Like many similar Zionist youth groups throughout the country, this group debated significant Jewish issues of the day.

PO'ALE ZION CLUB, 1917. The Po'ale Zion (Hebrew for "Workers of Zion") was organized in 1917 and later joined with Farband (the Jewish National Labor Alliance, later the Farband-Labor Zionist Order) to supply Palestine with tools. The group supported the Histadrut (the organization of trade unions in Palestine).

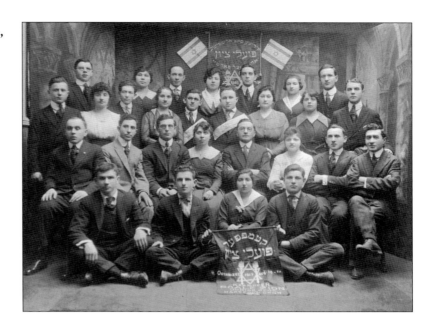

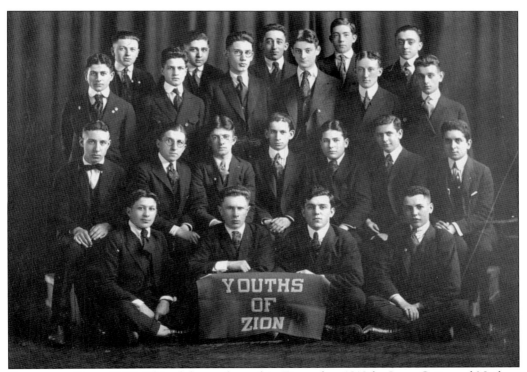

YOUTHS OF ZION, 1917. This club was formed in December 1912 by Leon Spitz and Nathan Cohen. The members, consisting of high school boys, were well known for their dramatic group, which put on many plays and sketches. Members also participated in many formal debates with other Zionist youth groups.

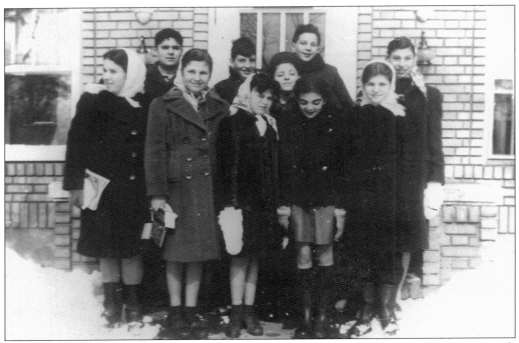

HABONIM TZOFIM, 1949. Habonim Tzofim was an educational and socialist Zionist youth movement that was founded in Great Britain in 1929. It soon spread to other English-speaking countries, which developed their own versions of the group. It was associated with the Labor Zionist movement and encouraged members to make *aliyah* to Israel. Here, members of the group stand in front of the Hebrew Children's Home.

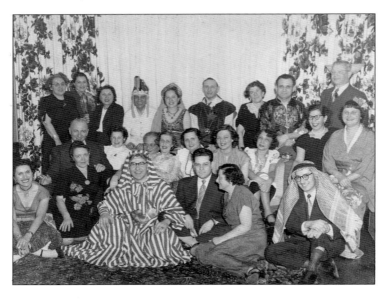

LABOR ZIONIST PARTY, 1935. The Labor Zionists were a secular group, as opposed to other Zionist organizations, which had a more religious focus and saw the creation of a Jewish homeland as the beginning of the Messianic era. The Labor Zionists were the left wing of the movement and believed that a Jewish state could only be realized if a strong Jewish working class settled in Palestine.

SAMUEL HOFFENBERG, 1972.
Samuel Hoffenberg (c. 1893–1987) was a prominent Zionist and Jewish community leader. The son of Rabbi Cemach Hoffenberg of Ados Israel Synagogue, he embraced Zionism at an early age, organizing the Youth Zionist Society in 1905. In 1910, he became the founder and first president of the Maccabaeans. As an adult, he was active in the Zionist Organization of America and founded or led 20 to 30 Jewish communal organizations.

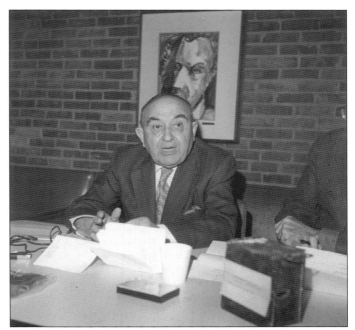

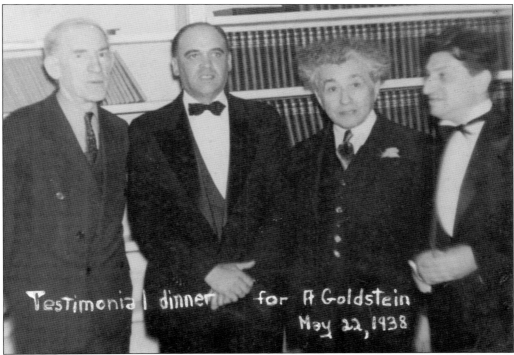

ABRAHAM GOLDSTEIN TESTIMONIAL DINNER, 1938. Born in Kiev, Abraham Goldstein (1893–1953), second from left, joined the Zionist movement as a schoolboy. In 1915, he fled the Russian army to come to America. In 1919, he moved to Hartford and worked for the Zionist Organization of America as Connecticut director. Able to speak eloquently in Yiddish, Goldstein built up chapters, brought in prominent speakers, and ultimately became an international Zionist leader.

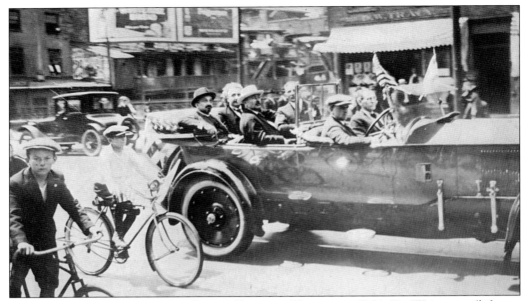

Dr. Chaim Weizmann and Dr. Albert Einstein, Hartford, 1921. Dr. Weizmann (left rear of car) and Dr. Einstein (right rear of car) came to Hartford in 1921 to raise money for Palestine. A parade with a motorcade of more than 500 cars was held, and approximately 15,000 spectators lined the streets. Following the parade, there was a dinner and mass meeting at the Capitol Theater, where $75,000 was raised for the Zionist cause.

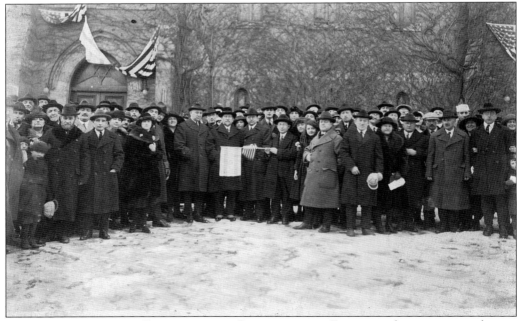

Zionist Conference at Emanuel, 1921. Participants in a Zionist conference are standing in front of The Emanuel Synagogue on Windsor Street in Hartford.

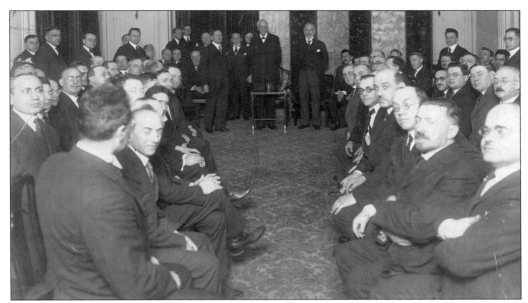

LORD BALFOUR VISITS THE UNITED STATES, 1921. In 1917, Lord Arthur James Balfour, Britain's foreign secretary, wrote a letter to Baron Lionel Walter Rothschild, one of Britain's foremost Jewish leaders, expressing the British government's support for a Jewish homeland in Palestine. Abraham Goldstein from Hartford (second from left) was a prominent Zionist activist.

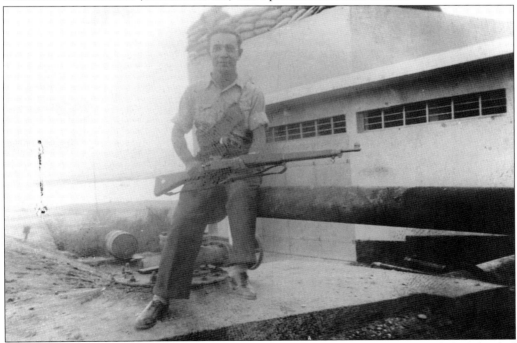

RABBI LINDENTHAL ON GUARD DUTY, PALESTINE, 1936. Born in Poland, Rabbi Haskel Lindenthal went to Palestine in the early 1930s to continue his education. He served in the Haganah (the pre-Israeli state underground military organization) for three and a half years. After immigrating to the United States, he became the rabbi of Teferes Israel Synagogue for many years.

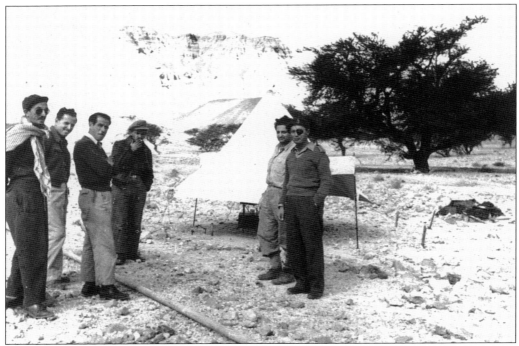

REUBEN PLEN, 1949. Reuben Plen (1922–2012), third from the left, stands near the first water pipe in Eilat, Israel, with Moshe Dayan, across on right. Plen served in the British army during World War II and then transferred to the Jewish Brigade. During Israel's War of Independence, he was in an engineering unit. In 1949, he was selected for Operation Arava, which built a road to Eilat with an airstrip and a government house.

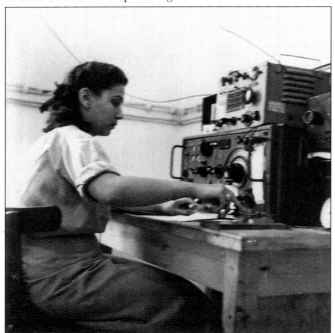

SARAH MARDER PLEN, 1949. Sarah Marder (1929–2005) was born in Hartford and went to Palestine after World War II. She served in the Haganah and was assigned to an attack unit guarding buses traveling to Jerusalem. She carried a concealed weapon under her clothes in case of attack. During Israel's 1948 War of Independence, Marder was a wireless operator for the Carmeli Brigade.

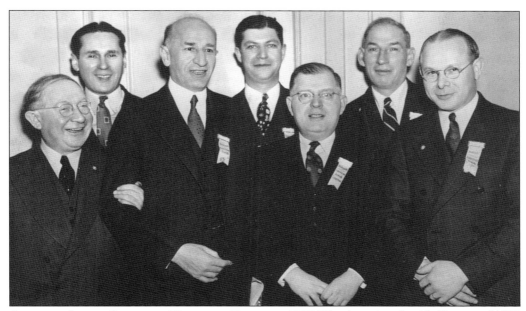

AMERICAN JEWISH CONGRESS, HARTFORD CHAPTER, 1937. The American Jewish Congress (AJC) began in 1918, with the goal of preserving the American way of life, promoting positive racial relationships, ensuring the survival of the Jewish people, and supporting Palestine. Hartford was one of the first national chapters. A strongly pro-Zionist entity, their goals often overlapped with the Zionist Organization of America, so the AJC focused more closely on rescuing European Jews.

NATIONAL UNITED JEWISH APPEAL MEETING, 1951. Standing in front of the table is Henry Montor (left), shaking hands with Samuel Roskin, campaign chairman for the Hartford Jewish Federation. David Ben-Gurion is seated second from the left. UJA was a philanthropic umbrella organization founded in 1939. It is now part of United Jewish Communities.

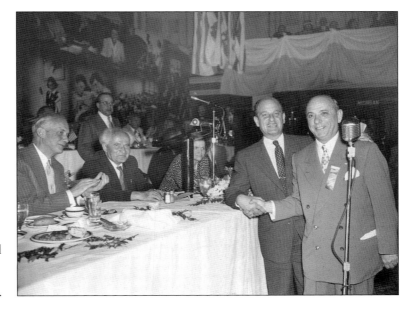

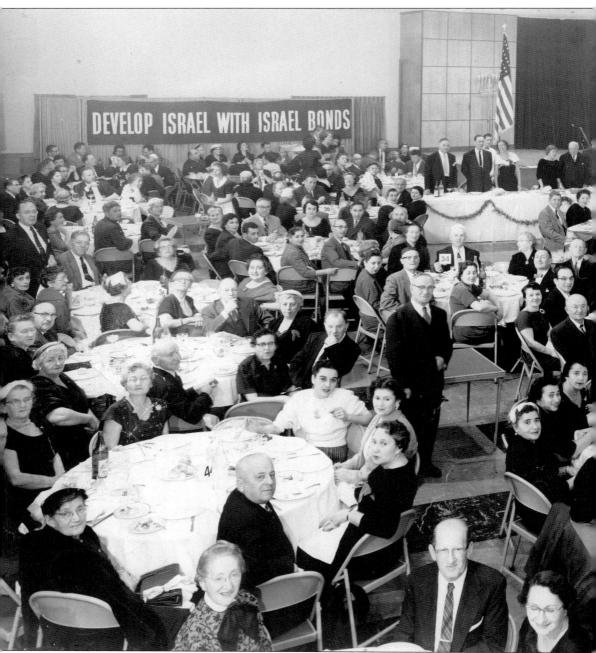

ISRAEL BONDS DINNER HONORING GOLDA MEIR, 1956. This Israel bonds dinner took place at Beth David Synagogue in West Hartford and featured Golda Meir, Israel's foreign minister. The Hartford community was strongly Zionist and brought many Israeli leaders to the area for fundraising. David Ben-Gurion conceived of selling Israel bonds in 1950 when he desperately needed funds for immigrant absorption and the development of a national infrastructure. Fundraising was

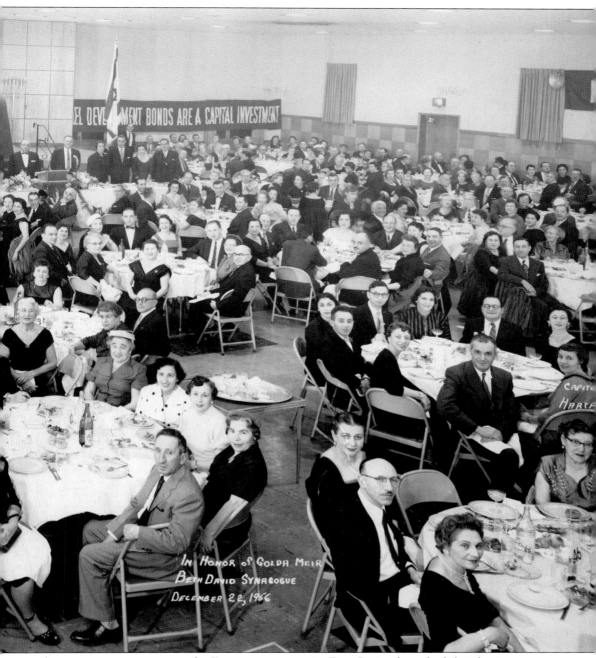

IN HONOR OF GOLDA MEIR
BETH DAVID SYNAGOGUE
DECEMBER 22, 1966

also seen as a way to engage the Diaspora community. Ben-Gurion broached the idea to a group of American leaders at a meeting in Jerusalem and launched the Development Corporation for Israel (DCI) at Madison Square Garden. The group expected to raise $25 million and actually raised $52 million. Sales are now global, and DCI continues to play a crucial role in Israel's economic development.

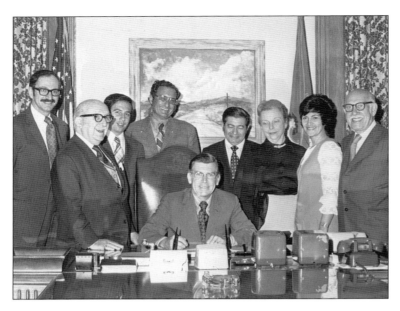

ISRAEL'S 25TH ANNIVERSARY, 1973. Gov. Thomas Meskill (seated) is surrounded by prominent members of the Jewish community as he signs a state proclamation in honor of Israel's 25th anniversary. From left to right are Alan Neves, Rabbi Abraham Feldman, Howard Klebanoff, Myron Yudkin, Berthold Gaster, Shirley Bunis, Natalie Rapaport, and Dr. Morris Cohen.

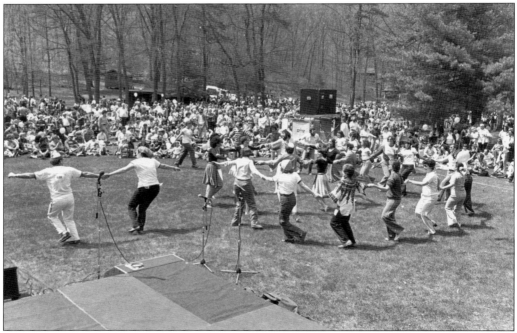

ISRAEL AT 30 CELEBRATION, 1978. The Hartford Jewish Federation and the Jewish Community Center often hold celebrations on the anniversary of Israel's independence. In 1978, the Jewish Federation celebrated Israel at 30 with a walkathon and dancing.

Five

COMMUNITY LIFE

Hartford's earliest Jewish settlers came from Germany and began to found mutual aid organizations that collected funds to provide benefits to their members. They were also deeply concerned about the welfare of the newer arrivals from Eastern Europe and created organizations to assist them in the Americanization process. At the same time, there was a deep economic and social divide between the groups. As the newcomers became more integrated into society, learning English and becoming more economically stable, these attitudes slowly began to change and improve. A strong desire to make life better for all Jews, here and abroad, especially those suffering in pogroms in Russia, helped to bring them together in 1912 to create United Jewish Charities, which was designed as a permanent agency to deal with the philanthropic needs of the community, such as support for the elderly, sick, and orphans, as well as providing young people with recreational and educational opportunities. Three leading rabbis brought together 30 different charitable groups to form this one entity, and the members raised $8,000 during its first year.

To facilitate fundraising and improve services, the Hartford Jewish Welfare Fund was formed in the late 1930s, and in 1940, the Jewish Community Council was established to work with and help coordinate the efforts of the many local organizations and agencies that continued to serve varying needs. In 1945, the Jewish Welfare Board and the Hartford Jewish Community Council merged, and the Hartford Jewish Federation (now known as the Jewish Federation of Greater Hartford) was formally incorporated by the state of Connecticut. The federation's stated purpose was "to coordinate, promote and advance the educational, cultural, social and philanthropic activities of the Jewish community; to raise and collect funds for distribution to and for the support of overseas, national and local Jewish nonprofit agencies; to undertake responsibility for central planning, coordination and administration of local Jewish welfare services to help safeguard and defend the civic, political and religious rights of the Jewish people." Today, more than 30 communal agencies receive support from the federation.

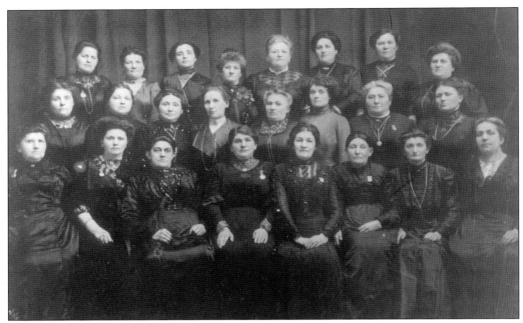

HEBREW HOME FOUNDERS, C. 1900 (ABOVE) AND RESIDENTS, 1980S (BELOW). In the late 1890s, a group of Orthodox women formed the Hebrew Ladies Sick Benefit Aid Association as a mutual aid society, with members donating $3 per week. In 1901, realizing that the group had amassed a large sum of money that their members were not using, they decided to create a home for the elderly. Visiting their neighbors, these women collected a nickel a week, which they carried in large handkerchiefs, leading to the name "the Handkerchief Brigade." After several moves due to growing need and expanding services, a new facility was built on Abrams Boulevard in West Hartford in 1989 and now is part of Hebrew Health Care.

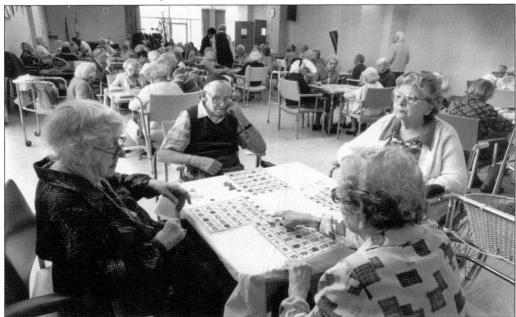

HEBREW LADIES OLD PEOPLE'S HOME, WOOSTER STREET, 1907. By 1907, the Hebrew Ladies Sick Benefit Aid Association had raised the money to purchase a house on Wooster Street. Volunteers cleaned, cooked, and cared for the residents. In 1929, a full-time superintendent and matron were hired, along with nurses who worked shifts to care for patients with more extensive medical needs. It was the first such facility in Connecticut.

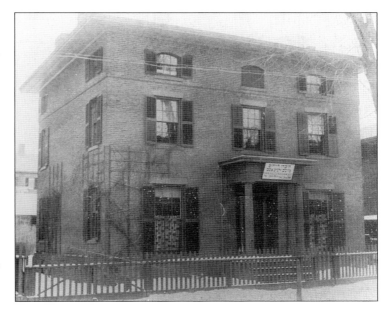

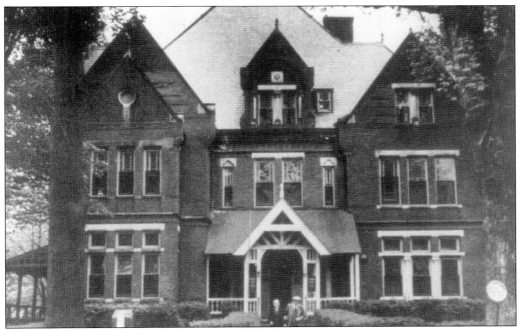

HEBREW HOME, WASHINGTON STREET, C. 1920S. Due to space needs, the Old People's Home's members raised funds to purchase the Hogle Mansion in 1919. It was remodeled to include a recreation hall, synagogue, and library. In 1925, an annex was added, but over time the population continued to grow, as did the need, and by the early 1950s, the community began raising funds to build a state-of-the-art facility.

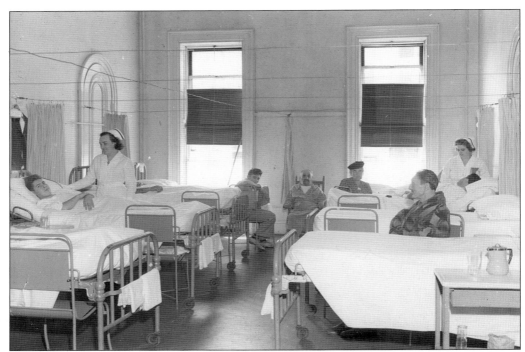

MOUNT SINAI, CAPITAL AVENUE, 1923. Mount Sinai Hospital opened in 1923 with 65 beds, and was one of the few Jewish-sponsored hospitals in the country at that time. Because Hartford Hospital and Saint Francis Hospital followed the accepted policy of denying admitting privileges to doctors they had not trained, Jewish physicians were prevented from admitting and visiting their own patients at either institution. Although most of Mount Sinai's doctors were Jewish, all patients were treated, regardless of race or religion. The hospital continued to grow and moved to a new building on Blue Hills Avenue in 1948, and more beds were added in 1959. The hospital continued to expand the facility and its services, merging with Saint Francis Hospital in 1989 to provide a broader level of care.

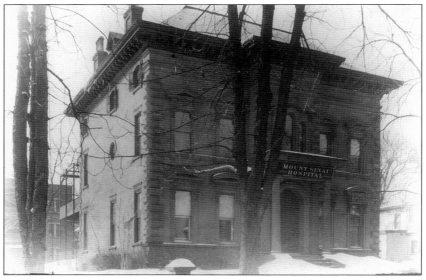

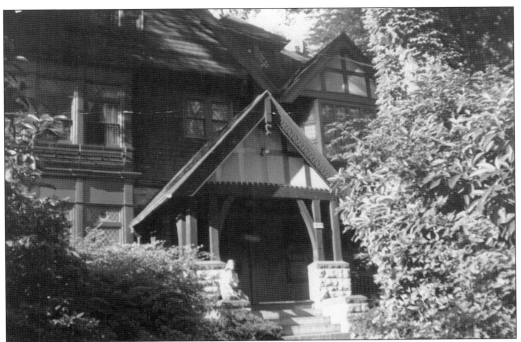

JEWISH COMMUNITY CENTER ON ASYLUM STREET, 1950S (ABOVE) AND BLOOMFIELD AVENUE IN WEST HARTFORD, 1970S (BELOW). In the early 1900s, youth activities were provided by the Young Men's and Young Women's Hebrew Associations, which offered Judaic studies along with social and athletic outlets. In 1928, they relocated to a different facility on Ann Street and operated there until 1935. This group disbanded in the late 1930s due to the Depression. During World War II, there was growing concern about the lack of activities for young people, so the Jewish Center Association was formed in 1942 on Vine Street. They ran after-school clubs and athletic programs there, as well as in parks and rented gyms. Fundraising efforts began in 1948 for a permanent home, and the Hartford Jewish Federation purchased a building on Asylum Avenue. The Jewish Community Center (JCC) began offering programming for seniors, preschoolers, and those with disabilities, along with art classes and musical and theatrical performances. To meet the growing demand, a new facility was built on Bloomfield Avenue in West Hartford in 1962.

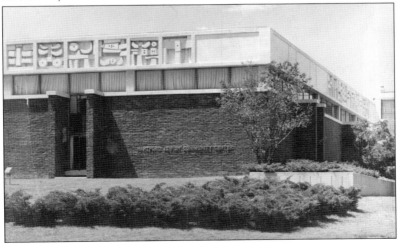

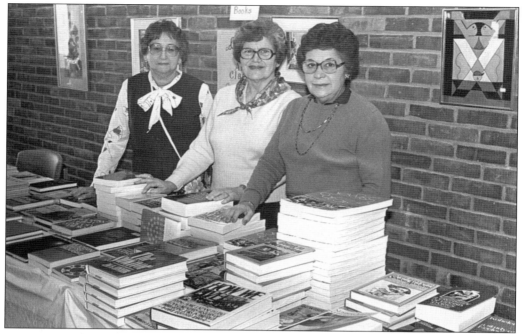

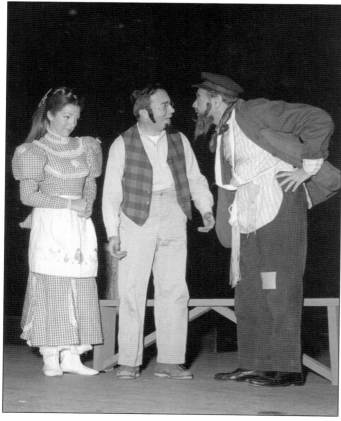

JCC Book Festival, 1980. For many years, the JCC celebrated Jewish Book Month by bringing prominent writers to the community, in conjunction with a sale of Jewish-themed books. In 1993, the Jewish Book Festival was created. It now hosts programs with well-known authors throughout the year.

JCC Center Players, 1965. The Center Players were the JCC's adult drama group. Their stated mission was to stage plays of Jewish interest, as well as revivals of classic international drama. Some of the group's performances included *Tevya and His Daughters* and *Of Mice and Men*. Along with these plays, the JCC also frequently hosted productions sponsored by the Ann Randall Arts Committee and youth theater groups.

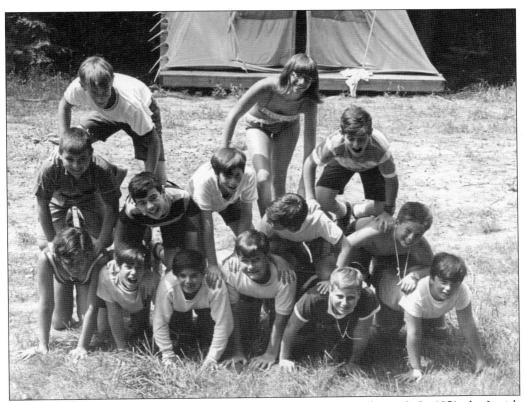

CAMP SHALOM CAMPERS, 1968 (ABOVE) AND DINING HALL, 1978 (BELOW). In 1951, the Jewish Children's Service Organization purchased 100 acres of land in New Hartford, Connecticut, for a day camp and deeded it to the Jewish Community Center. In 1952, it was dedicated as Camp Shalom, remaining there until a new location with more space and additional facilities was needed. The camp moved to Windsor, Connecticut, in 1978. Among Camp Shalom's many innovations was a program for integrating children with disabilities into the regular camp activities. Over the years, it has also hosted many Jewish conferences and community gatherings.

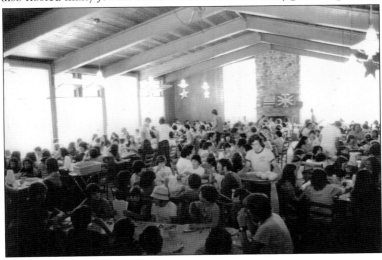

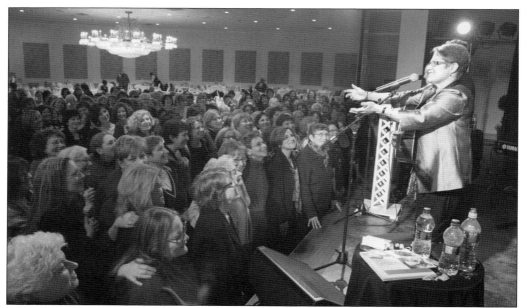

WOMEN'S SEDER, 2010. This 2010 Women's Seder was led by nationally known singer/songwriter Debbie Friedman, who performed her music, along with readings by a number of women rabbis, cantors, and community leaders. The event, sponsored by the Mandell Jewish Community Center, brought together over 500 women to create a spiritual and meaningful Passover celebration. (Courtesy of the Mandell Jewish Community Center.)

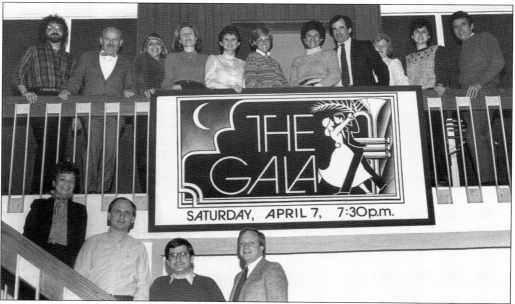

JCC GALA, 1986. Beginning in 1983, the JCC held an annual fundraising event called the Gala. The initial event was a musical revue, which later expanded to include dinner, dancing, auctions, and more. The money raised went to the JCC's scholarship program, which provided financial assistance to those who could not afford summer camp, nursery school, and other JCC programs.

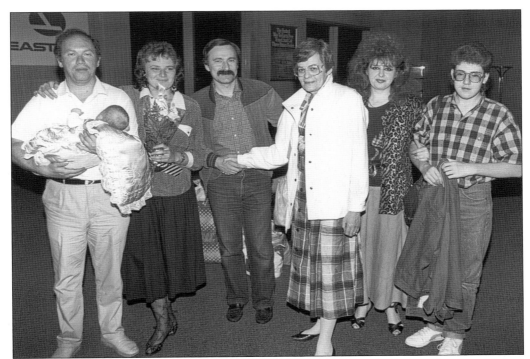

New Americans with Jewish Family Services, 1988. Jewish Family Services began as United Jewish Charities. In 1940, the name changed to United Jewish Social Services, and in 1968 became Jewish Family Services. Today, it has expanded into a multi-faceted agency that provides a wide variety of services, including counseling and psychological services for adults and children, employment transition support, Holocaust survivor assistance, and a kosher food pantry.

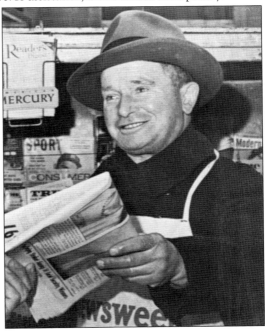

Jewish Community Foundation, 1976. In the late 1960s, the Hartford Jewish Federation proposed a separate organization to support projects, assist the federation financially, and contribute to non-sectarian causes. After accumulating seed money, the Jewish Community Foundation opened in 1972. Today, it collects and invests community funds and provides grants for Jewish and secular agencies as well as specialized programs. Max Pivnik (1903–1958), a Hartford newsstand owner, established a philanthropic fund in 1976.

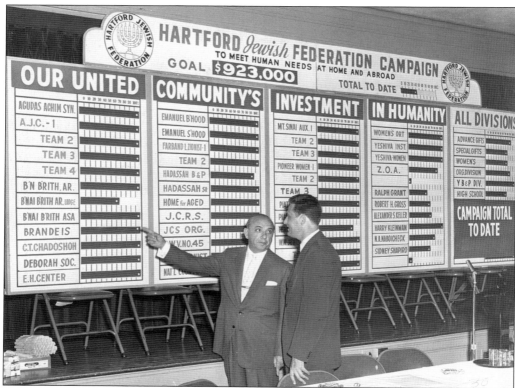

HARTFORD JEWISH FEDERATION EVENTS, 1956 (ABOVE) AND 1978 (BELOW). In 1945, the Jewish Federation was created after 15 years of planning. This work began in the 1930s with the Hartford Jewish Council, under the auspices of United Jewish Charities, which combined 30 charitable groups. The goal was to coordinate the work of various charities, as well as their often overlapping fundraising efforts. A report was issued, and the Hartford Jewish Welfare Fund was established to conduct all future drives. In 1940, a total of 62 affiliated organizations formed the Jewish Community Council. In 1945, the Jewish Welfare Fund and the Jewish Community Council merged, creating the Hartford Jewish Federation. The federation not only raises funds for the local Jewish community and its organizations, but also contributes to international Jewish and non-Jewish causes and is a staunch advocate and supporter of Israel.

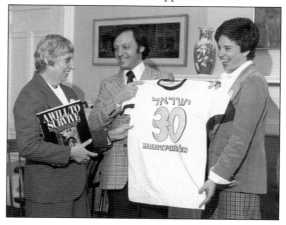

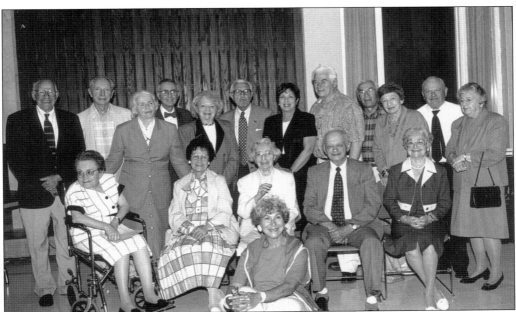

JEWISH HISTORICAL SOCIETY OF GREATER HARTFORD FOUNDERS, C. 1991 (ABOVE) AND EXHIBIT, 2007 (BELOW). The idea for a historical society to collect and preserve Hartford's Jewish history started in the late 1960s. The first meeting was held in 1971, with Emma Cohen as the first president. Soon, volunteers began conducting oral history interviews and collecting archival materials. The federation made a small space available for an office and eventually a paid executive director was hired to run operations, maintain and increase the archival collection, and create programming, exhibits, and publications. The society is dedicated to collecting and preserving historical documents, photographs, and memorabilia of the Jewish community of Greater Hartford, and its goal is to reach the largest audience possible through publications, exhibitions, seminars, and educational programs.

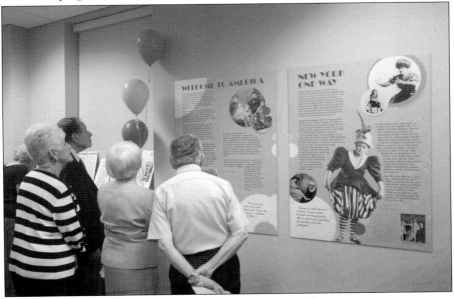

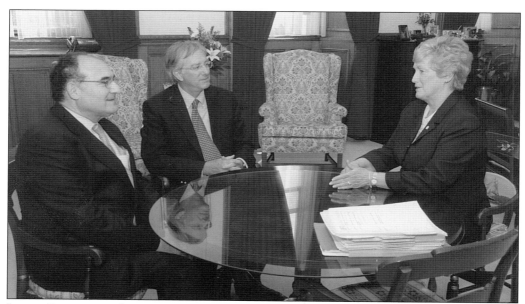

JEWISH FEDERATION ASSOCIATION OF CONNECTICUT WITH GOV. JODI RELL (RIGHT), 2007. The Jewish Federation Association of Connecticut (JFACT) is the government and community relations arm of the Jewish Federation system in Connecticut. It advocates and lobbies for the Jewish community and Israel, while also collaborating with interfaith and secular nonprofit and social service agencies to assist the needy. (Courtesy of JFACT.)

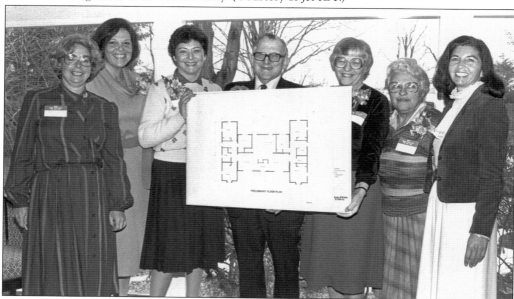

JEWISH ASSOCIATION FOR COMMUNITY LIVING GROUP HOME, 1981. This organization, formerly the Committee for the Developmentally Disabled, became a federation beneficiary agency in the early 1980s. Their mission is to assist "people with developmental disabilities to participate in community life through personal empowerment, community engagement, family relationships, and quality services, enhanced by Jewish tradition." The group home accepts people of all faiths and backgrounds.

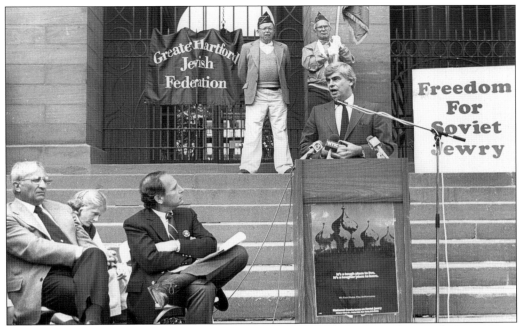

JEWISH COMMUNITY RELATIONS COUNCIL SOVIET JEWRY RALLY, 1985. The Jewish Community Relations Council (JCRC) is the non-partisan public affairs voice of the Jewish Federation of Greater Hartford. JCRC speaks out on issues of public policy, advocates for political legislative initiatives, and is committed to social justice and to protecting and strengthening Jewish life locally, in Israel, and throughout the world.

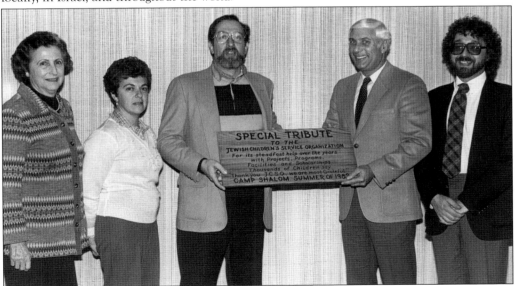

JEWISH CHILDREN'S SERVICE ORGANIZATION, 1981. The Jewish Children's Service Organization was founded in 1950 as an outgrowth of the Hebrew Home for Children. It raises funds to offer scholarships and other types of financial and practical assistance for children. In 1951, it purchased land in New Hartford for the Jewish Community Center to use as a day camp. In 1978, that location was sold and the camp was relocated to Windsor, Connecticut.

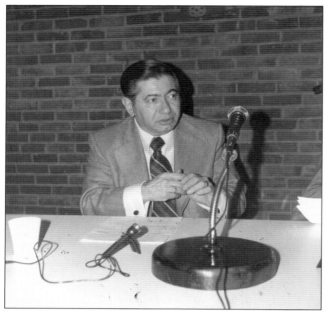

BERTHOLD GASTER, CONNECTICUT JEWISH LEDGER, 1977. Publishers Samuel Neusner and Frank Dubinsky founded the *Connecticut Jewish Ledger* in 1929 with Rabbi Abraham Feldman as editor. Dubinsky soon resigned and Frederick Neusner became executive vice president. It was purchased in 1967 by Berthold Gaster and Shirley Bunis, both longtime employees. Although there are no longer separate regional editions, the *Ledger* remains a primary source for local Jewish community news under new ownership.

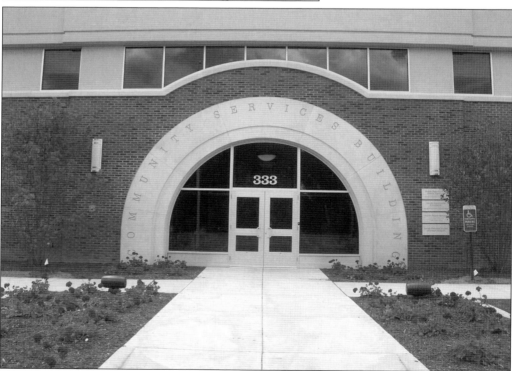

COMMUNITY SERVICES BUILDING, BLOOMFIELD AVENUE, 2004. The Community Services Building was dedicated on June 11, 2006. This brought together the Jewish Federation of Greater Hartford, the Jewish Historical Society of Greater Hartford, Jewish Family Services, and the Jewish Community Foundation of Greater Hartford under one roof and created a campus with the Mandell Jewish Community Center and the nearby Hebrew Health Care.

Six

SOCIAL AND CIVIC CLUBS AND ORGANIZATIONS

Jews in Hartford created many of their own fraternal and charitable organizations, but they also joined established American groups, such as the Odd Fellows and Masonic lodges. In 1851, a group of German Jews established the Ararat Lodge, a local chapter of B'nai B'rith, a national organization founded in 1843. It was the 13th chapter in the United States, and at first, German was the official language of the meetings. The lodge was secular and devoted to the social and philanthropic interests of its members. It also offered aid to members in the form of sick and death benefits and unemployment compensation, which were crucial at a time when there was no government "safety net." In time, the group's charitable efforts expanded, and members contributed to both Jewish and non-Jewish causes.

Jews also became politically active, and by 1864, there were three Jews elected to Hartford's City Council. They also served on many city and state-wide committees, such as the 1852 Fourth of July celebration committee. Several were prominent on the national stage, such as Sen. Herman Kopplemann, who was a congressman in the 1930s and 1940s, and Abraham Ribicoff, Connecticut's first Jewish governor, who was active in politics from the 1950s through the early 1980s.

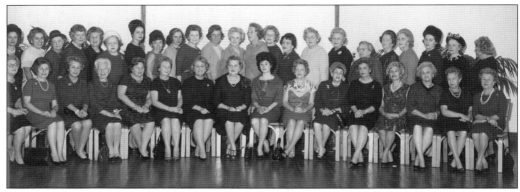

DEBORAH SOCIETY, C. 1960S (ABOVE) AND 1974 (BELOW). Originally called Frauen Verein (German for "women's organization"), it was founded in 1852 by German Jewish women from Congregation Beth Israel, and its constitution and bylaws were written in German. With no national affiliation, it was the first independent Jewish women's group in the country. The name changed to Deborah Society in 1854. Members performed religious, social, and philanthropic activities for the congregation and the community, and were entitled to medical services, financial assistance, and a widow's stipend. They visited the sick, sewed for the poor, and distributed clothing. Members also sewed funeral shrouds and washed and dressed the dead until the congregation became Reform. The organization supported Civil War relief and aided victims of the 1906 San Francisco earthquake and fire, among many other charitable efforts through the years. It disbanded in the late 1980s.

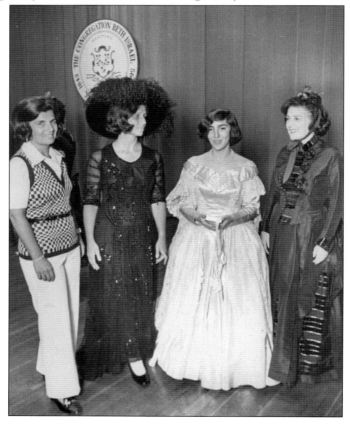

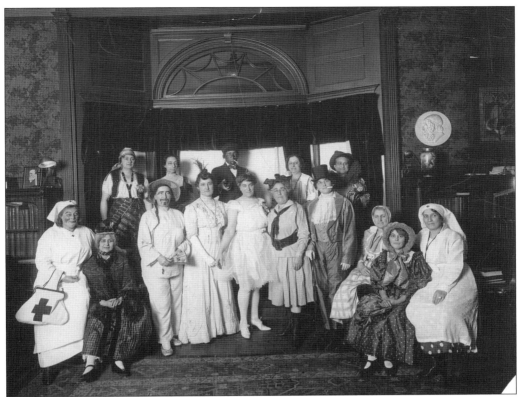

THE FIFTEEN CLUB, CONGREGATION BETH ISRAEL, C. 1910s. The Fifteen Club was organized in 1886 with 15 women at the initial meeting. For many years, their Purim Ball was the most important Jewish social event in Hartford and featured both music and elaborate costumes. The club raised money for Hartford's Hebrew Widows and Orphans Society as well as for general causes, such as Camp Courant.

YENTA'S FOLLIES, 1947. Yenta's Follies was a production of the Mr. and Mrs. Club of The Emanuel Synagogue. It was a variety show consisting of sketches and musical numbers in two acts. The production was presented annually at Weaver High School in the late 1940s and 1950s as a fundraiser for the club.

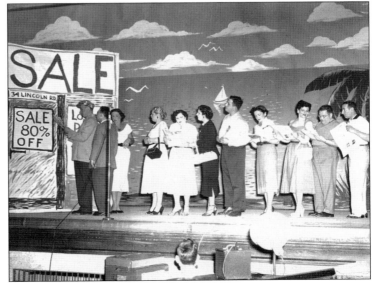

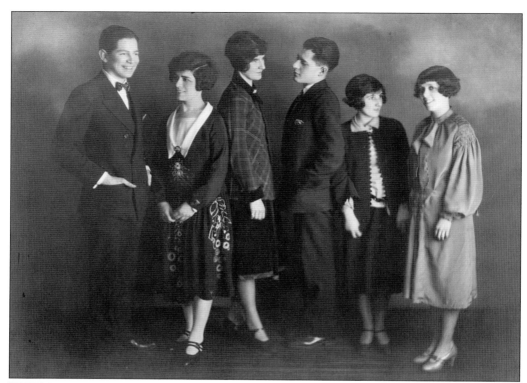

YWHA BLACK AND WHITE REVUE, 1920S (ABOVE) AND JR. YMHA, 1920–1922 (BELOW). The Black and White Revue, run by the YWHA, was a variety show created by Mindel Borden in 1920. The first production took place in 1922, with 130 men and women in the cast and more than 1,400 people attending. The revue ran successfully for a number of years in various locations. The YMHA was first organized as a social club in 1917, but in 1919 changed its emphasis to education of Jewish and communal issues. It continued to develop social, recreation, and athletic programming.

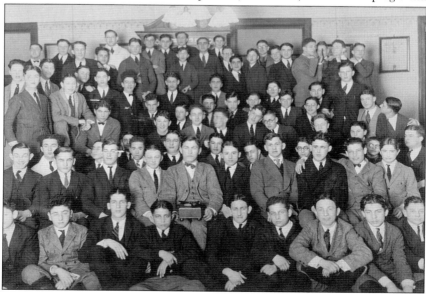

HADASSAH BOARD MEMBERS, 1930. Hadassah is one of the world's largest Jewish organizations. In 1914, its founder, Henrietta Szold, came to Hartford to help launch a local chapter, which still exists today. By 1949, local membership had risen to 3,000. Hadassah raised money to buy land in Palestine and shipped clothing and other necessities there. It now runs medical and educational facilities in Israel and serves people of all religions and nationalities.

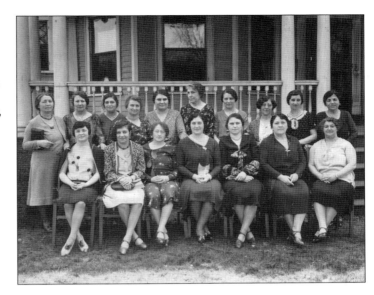

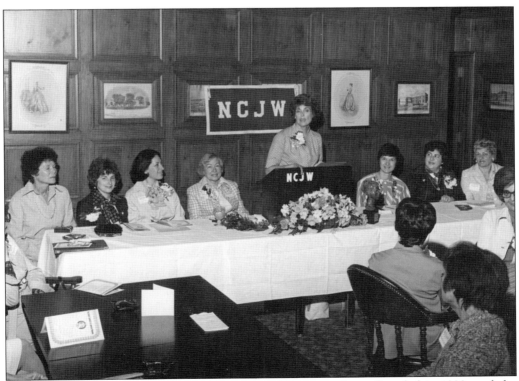

NATIONAL COUNCIL OF JEWISH WOMEN, 1970s. The council was founded in 1893, and the Hartford chapter was established in 1910. It aided immigrants and sponsored Americanization classes. The council safely housed Jewish working women, and a "milk station" provided milk for poor infants. In addition, it offered educational scholarships and funded many social service projects. The Hartford chapter promotes interfaith programming and supports legislation for social improvement.

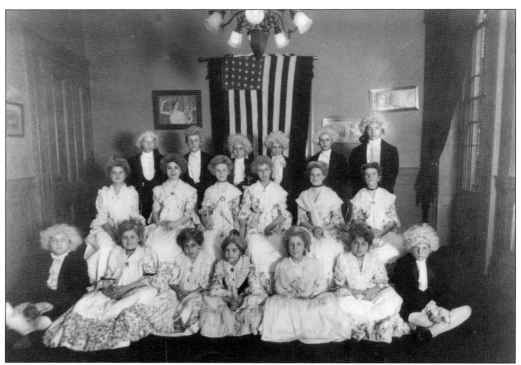

TOURO CLUB, 1910 (ABOVE) AND TUMBLE BROOK COUNTRY CLUB, 1975 (BELOW). Tumble Brook Country Club was incorporated in 1922 as an outgrowth of the Touro Club. The Touro Club was a social organization established in 1901 with membership limited to German Jews, although this barrier was later lifted and Eastern European Jews were admitted. After facing discrimination at local country clubs, the group purchased land in Bloomfield for a nine-hole golf course. A large clubhouse opened in 1924, and the golf course later expanded. Tumble Brook has often been used for elegant social events sponsored by the Jewish Federation of Greater Hartford, including the annual Ambassador's Ball (pictured below).

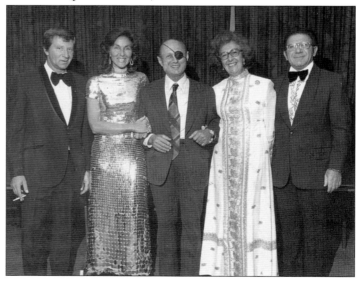

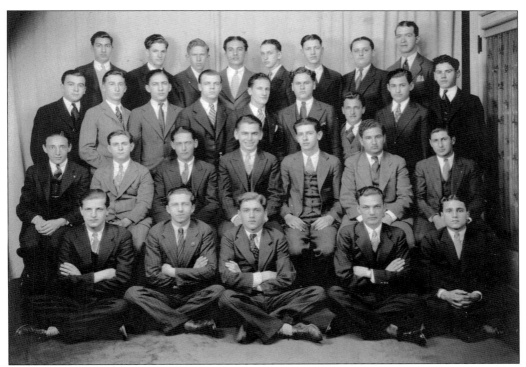

B'NAI B'RITH ARARAT LODGE, 1929 (ABOVE) AND 1971 (BELOW). B'nai B'rith, the nation's oldest Jewish fraternal organization, was founded in New York City in 1843 by German Jews seeking to unite Jews of various religious denominations. Hartford's Ararat Lodge, established in 1851, also served social, cultural, and philanthropic purposes. Dues and donations provided sick benefits, unemployment compensation, and life insurance, as well as religious education for members' children. In Hartford, social prestige was associated with membership, which was initially limited to German Jews. Bylaws and minutes were written in German until 1882. Subsequently, when Eastern European Jews joined, English became the common language. Members were active in Jewish life locally and worldwide. Over the years, funds were donated to Israel, colleges and universities, local charities, and a variety of other causes.

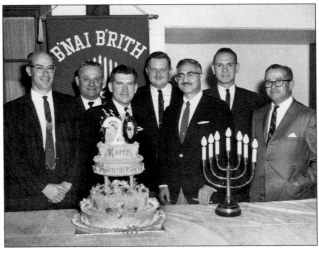

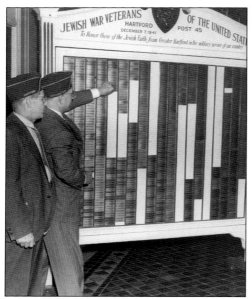

JEWISH WAR VETERANS, 1940S. This group began in 1896 as the Jewish Civil War Veterans. In 1929, they became known as the Jewish War Veterans of the United States of America. Hartford Post No. 45 was founded in the 1930s, and Laurel Post No. 394 in 1946. They merged in 1953, and in 2014, the name was changed to the Sgt. John L. Levitow Post No. 45.

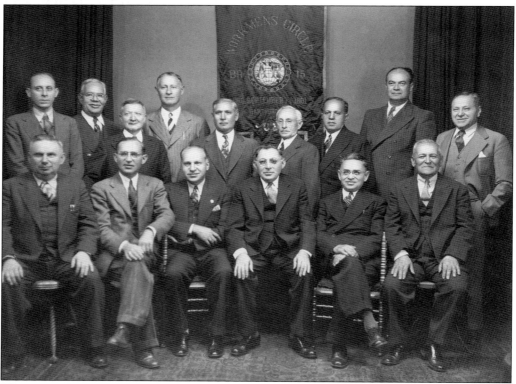

WORKMEN'S CIRCLE BRANCH 15, 1941. Originally founded in New York City in 1900, the Workman's Circle ("Der Arbeiter Ring" in German) was a Socialist organization that provided extensive services to its members. Hartford Branch No. 15 was founded in 1901, and other branches soon followed, eventually coming together as the Workmen's Circle Educational Alliance. In 1927, the Ladies Club was formed. In the 1970s, many branches dissolved.

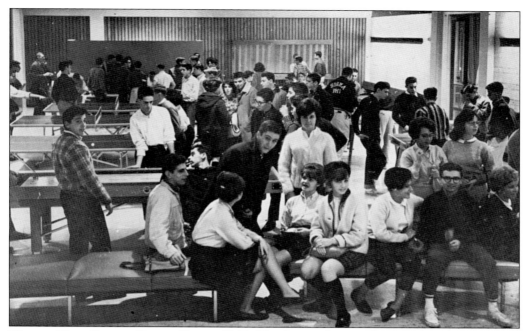

WEAVER HIGH SCHOOL SOCIAL CLUBS, 1963. The first graduating class at Weaver High School was in 1924. Weaver was considered an example of one of America's best high schools. Throughout the years, some of the clubs at Weaver included the Dramatic Club, the Chess Club, the Boys' Commercial Club, the Girls' Leaders' Corp, and the Caroline Hewins Literary Society.

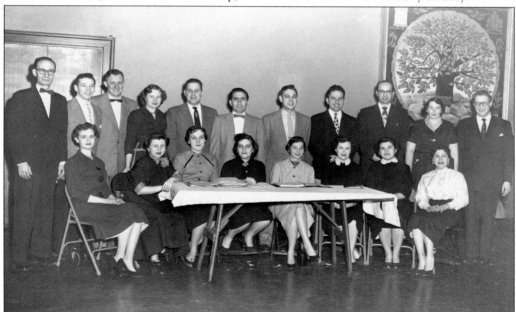

MR. AND MRS. CLUB, AGUDAS ACHIM, C. 1940S. The Mr. and Mrs. Club of Agudas Achim Synagogue got its start in 1954 from the Double A Club, also known as the Agudas Achim Social Club. With more of the social club's members getting married, the members felt the need for a group that catered specifically to married couples.

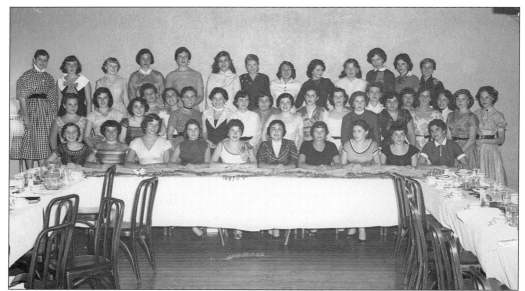

PHI DELTA SORORITY, WEAVER HIGH SCHOOL, C. 1953. This sorority was a sisterhood dedicated to promoting charitable functions. Since this period coincided with a migration to the suburbs, the group became important in maintaining friendships, which helped sustain these young women during their transition, since they could remain members even after they stopped attending Weaver.

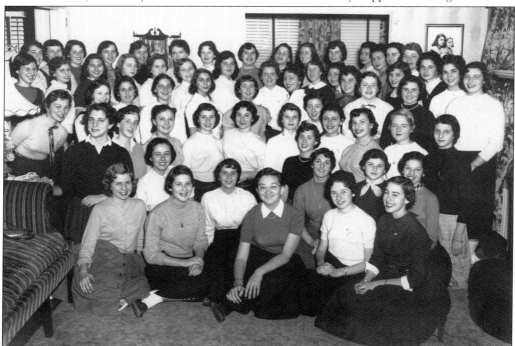

IOTA PHI SORORITY, 1955. This chapter consisted of girls from Weaver and Hall High Schools. They met one evening a week in a member's home. An annual dance and ad journal raised money for local charities. "Our time spent together were the best days of our youth," one member recalls. (Courtesy of Barbara Siskin.)

B'NAI B'RITH GIRLS, WEAVER HIGH, 1950s. In 1941, the Women's Supreme Council of B'nai B'rith adopted the name B'nai B'rith Girls (BBG), and in 1944, when B'nai B'rith officially recognized BBG, the B'nai B'rith Youth Organization (BBYO) was born. This club for teenage girls emphasizes community service, leadership, Jewish education, and the importance of Israel. In 2002, BBYO became an independent organization.

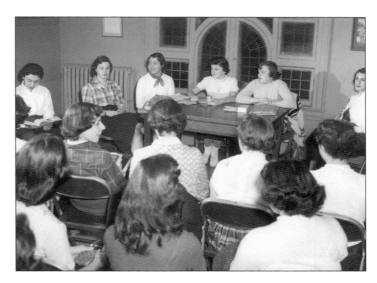

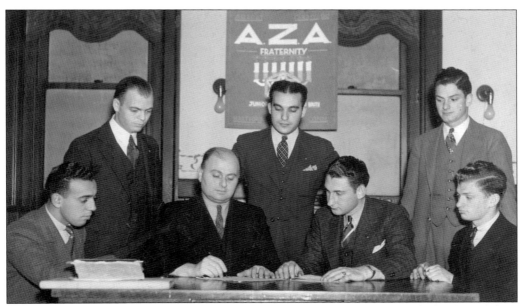

B'NAI B'RITH AZA, 1935. AZA (Aleph Zadik Aleph) began in 1923 with the first club in Omaha, Nebraska. In 1924, it was declared an international order, and in 1925, it was adopted by B'nai B'rith International. The group is pluralistic and open to teenage boys in grades nine through twelve. AZA emphasizes leadership training, community service, Jewish education, and a commitment to Israel.

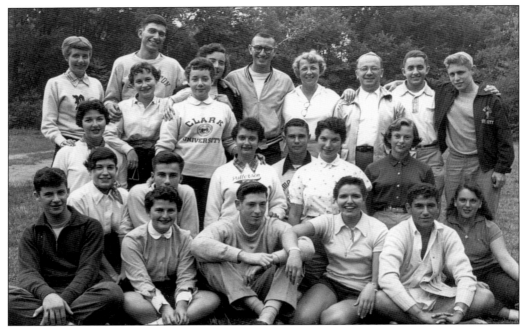

CONNECTICUT REGION UNITED SYNAGOGUE YOUTH CONCLAVE, 1954. United Synagogue Youth is the youth movement of the United Synagogue of Conservative Judaism. Founded in 1951, its purpose is to bring Jewish teenagers closer to Judaism and Israel through educational and social programming. Hartford chapters belonged to the Connecticut Valley Region for many years and are now part of the Hanefesh Region, consisting of chapters throughout Connecticut and western Massachusetts.

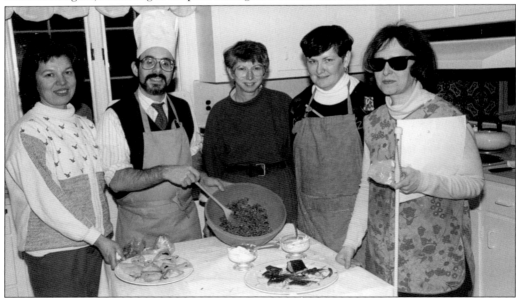

EMANUEL SISTERHOOD, 1989. The Emanuel Sisterhood was formed in 1919 as an auxiliary when the synagogue was established. Annie Fisher served as its first president. Many synagogues have sisterhood organizations, which provide financial and physical support to their congregations, along with cultural and social activities for members.

Seven

NOTABLE MENTIONS

Hartford was the home of numerous individuals who became well-known in their chosen professions. Some came to the city from Eastern Europe as young children or had parents who were immigrants. Many remembered their Hartford roots and frequently returned to the city to visit or raise funds for local organizations. Several, such as singer Sophie Tucker, are buried in local synagogue cemeteries. Because it is impossible to include all of Hartford's famous Jewish sons and daughters, only a select few who have become prominent on a national level are discussed in this chapter.

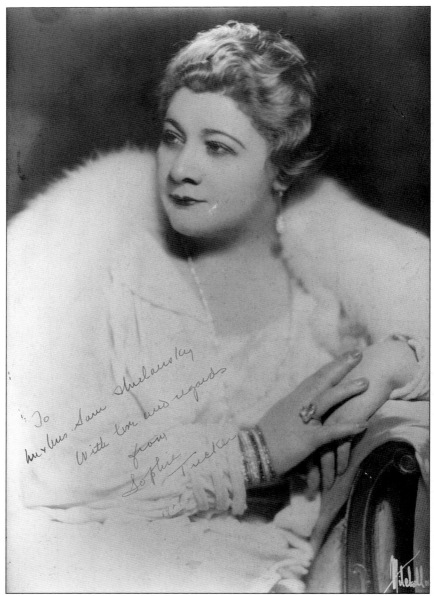

SOPHIE TUCKER, 1929. Sophie Tucker (1884–1966) was born Sonya Kalish, but her father, fleeing Russian authorities, changed the family's name to Abuza. They settled in Hartford and opened a restaurant. As a girl, she waited tables and sang popular tunes for tips. After a brief marriage, she went to New York seeking fame, changed her name to Sophie Tucker, and began performing in vaudeville. After signing with the William Morris Agency, she appeared in cabarets and on Broadway. Tucker became known as "the Last of the Red Hot Mammas" for her slightly risqué act, but one of her most famous songs was the sentimental "My Yiddish Momma." Changing with the times, she made movies, sang in nightclubs, and appeared on television, especially on *The Ed Sullivan Show*. She was known to be kind and gracious to her fellow performers and behind-the-scenes-workers and assisted many in their career goals. She was also a generous philanthropist who donated to various charities, including a few local Jewish institutions.

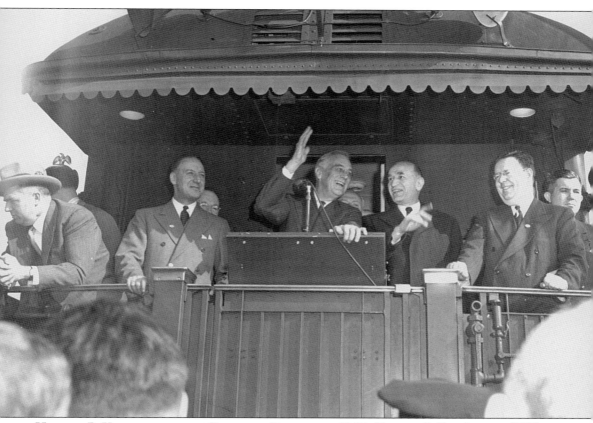

HERMAN P. KOPPLEMANN WITH PRESIDENT ROOSEVELT, 1940. Herman P. Kopplemann (1880–1957), third from right, came from Russia in 1882 and started a business at the age of eight selling newspapers. He established a successful newspaper and magazine distribution firm despite only finishing one year of school at Hartford Public High School. A Democrat, Kopplemann began his political involvement in his teens and was elected to the Board of Aldermen despite the fact that he was below the voting age, then 21, at the time. A few years later, he became a member of the Hartford City Council, becoming its president in 1911. In 1932, he became the first Jewish congressman from Connecticut and was reelected to five nonconsecutive terms. Though Kopplemann was a businessman, he ardently supported social reforms throughout his political career, including Roosevelt's New Deal, which he saw as good for business. He looked out for the poor and disadvantaged and fought equally against segregation and the power of the big banks. He advocated for the Jewish community in Hartford and beyond and served on the boards of local Jewish organizations.

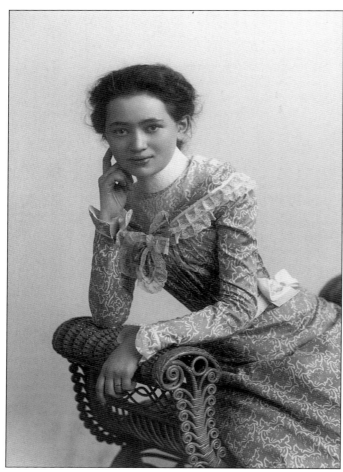

ANNIE FISHER, C. 1900 (LEFT) AND 1934 (BELOW). Annie Fisher (1883–1968) came to America as a young child and received a scholarship to attend Wesleyan University. She returned to Hartford to teach, beginning with adult English classes in the evening, and eventually found a full-time job at a school with a largely non–English speaking population. She had a strong interest in special-needs children and immigrants and designed specialized educational and testing programs to accommodate them. She became the first female district supervisor and also the first female principal in Hartford. She introduced free dental care, free glasses, and shower facilities in schools. Fisher also involved herself in reforming salaries and pensions for teachers. After her retirement, a Hartford elementary school was named in her honor.

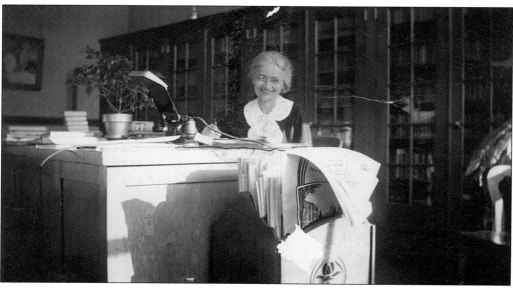

HAROLD ROME, 1950 (RIGHT) AND 1974 (BELOW). Harold Rome (1908–1993) was a composer, lyricist, and writer for musical theater. He studied at the Yale University School of Architecture and covered his expenses by performing in nightclubs and dance halls. Unable to find an architectural job due to the Depression, he began writing arrangements for bands at Jewish summer resorts. He was asked to write songs for *Pins and Needles*, a revue being produced by the International Ladies Garment Workers Union. This became the longest-running musical of the 1930s. During World War II, Rome was a member of Army Special Services entertaining the troops and wrote for George Kaufman and Moss Hart. His Broadway musicals include *Fanny* and *Destry Rides Again*. (Right, photograph by Carl Van Vechten, courtesy of the Van Vechten Trust and the Yale Collection of American Literature, Beinecke Library; below, courtesy of Joshua Rome.)

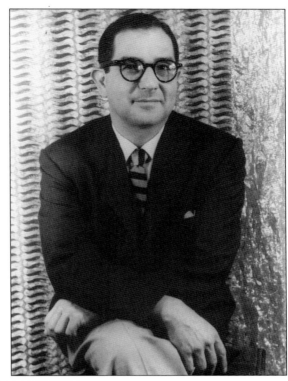

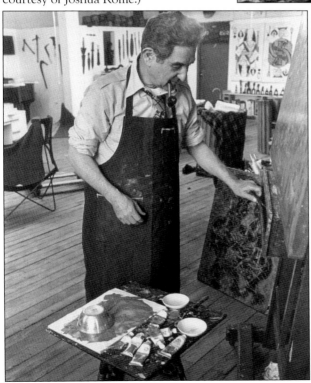

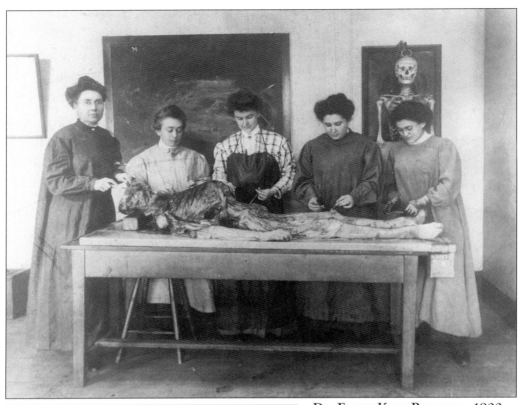

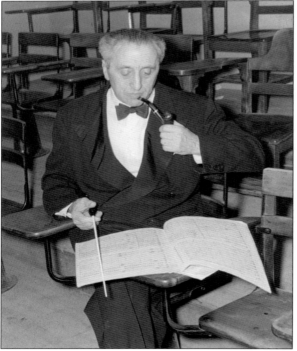

DR. FANNY KARP RADOM, C. 1900.
Fanny Karp Radom (1876–1948),
second from left, was the first female
physician on the medical staff of
Mount Sinai Hospital. She was also
one of the first women to be licensed
as a pharmacist in Connecticut
and served as a physician for 30
years. Throughout her career she
faced the ongoing challenge of
gender and religious prejudices.

DR. MOSHE PARANOV, 1956. Born
Morris Perelmutter, Moshe Paranov
(1895–1994) was considered a musical
prodigy and often performed in
local synagogues. In 1920, he joined
Julius Hartt, one of his teachers, to
found the Hartt School of Music
and was its first director after it
affiliated with the University of
Hartford. He often brought famous
artists like Isaac Stern to the
school. He was also co-conductor
of the Hartford Symphony.

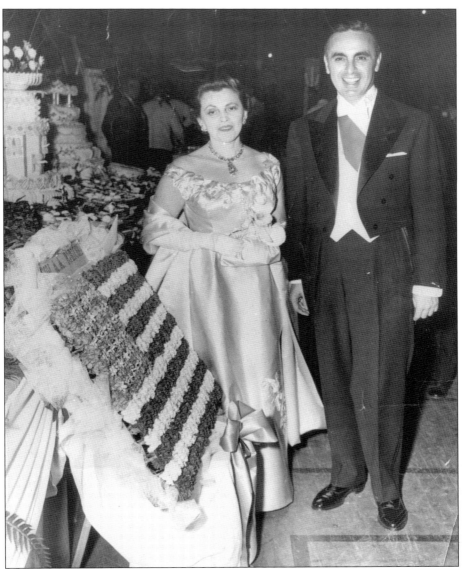

ABRAHAM "ABE" AND RUTH RIBICOFF, 1955. Abe Ribicoff (1910–1998) grew up in New Britain, the son of Orthodox immigrants. The anti-Catholic sentiment against presidential candidate Al Smith in 1928 had a profound influence on him and inspired a lifelong fight against prejudice. After receiving his law degree from the University of Chicago, he returned to Hartford and became involved with local politics. A liberal Democrat, he served in the Connecticut legislature and was elected to Congress in 1949. Ribicoff lost the 1952 Senate race to Prescott Bush, but despite an anti-Semitic backlash late in the race, he was elected the state's first Jewish governor in 1954. As governor, he responded to the 1955 flood and also proposed tough penalties for speeding and drunk driving. Ribicoff later joined Pres. John F. Kennedy's cabinet as secretary of health, education and welfare. He won a Senate seat in 1962 and served several terms. Ribicoff gave a memorable speech at the 1968 Democratic convention, condemning police brutality against anti-Vietnam protestors, and worked with the Carter administration for peace in the Middle East. He retired from politics in 1981.

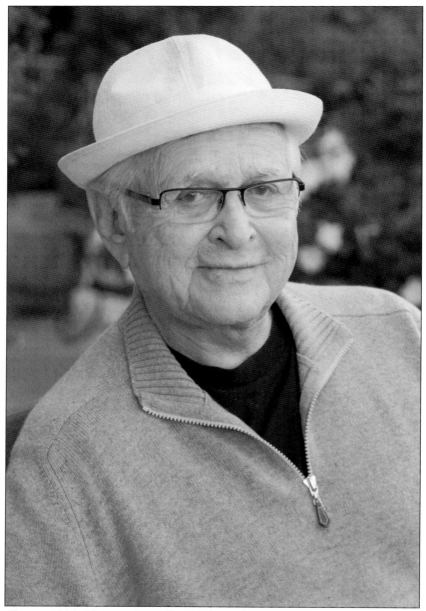

NORMAN LEAR, 2014. Norman Lear (b. 1922) was born in New Haven, but his family later moved to Hartford, and he attended Weaver High School. After World War II, he moved to Los Angeles to work in public relations. He became a producer in 1959, after creating a series for Henry Fonda. CBS liked his idea for a show about a blue-collar family, and in 1971, *All in the Family* began airing. His other television productions include *Sanford and Son, Maude, The Jeffersons, One Day at a Time, Good Times,* and *Mary Hartman, Mary Hartman.* These shows broke new ground by dealing with the social and political issues of the day in a remarkably frank manner. In 1984, he was inducted into the Television Academy Hall of Fame. During his career, he won four Emmys and a Peabody Award. In 1999, Pres. Bill Clinton awarded him a National Medal of Arts. (Courtesy of Norman Lear.)

MIKE KELLIN, 1981. Born Myron Kellin, Mike Kellin (1922–1983) served in the military during World War II and then studied acting and playwriting at the Yale University School of Drama. Because of his rugged features, he was often cast in "tough guy" roles. Kellin appeared in 50 plays and won an Obie for *American Buffalo*. He also appeared in numerous movie and television productions.

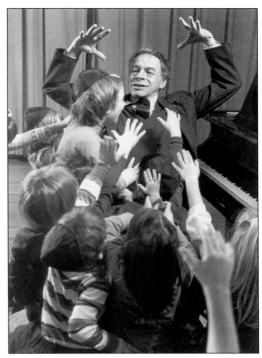

ANN RANDALL, 1956. Ann Randall (1908–1961) was a Broadway performer before returning to Hartford. She was the founder of the Randall School for Dramatic Arts and head of the Drama Department of the Hartford Conservatory. She was also the force behind the Cultural Arts Committee at the Jewish Community Center. Her students included Ernest Borgnine, Ted Knight, and Norman Lear.

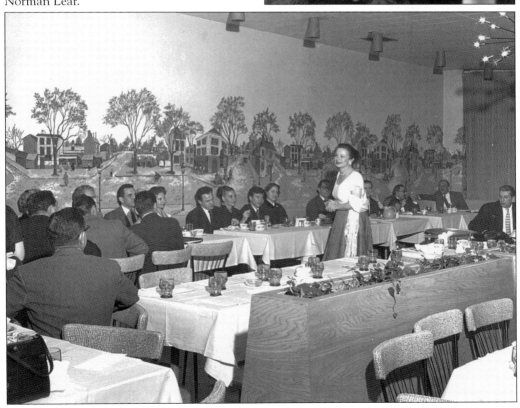

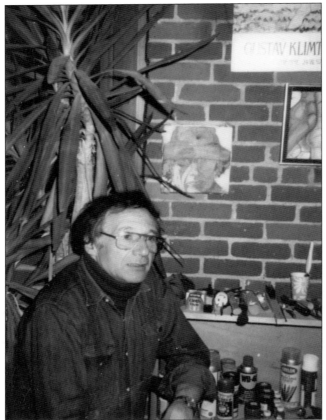

ELBERT WEINBERG (LEFT) AND THE HOLOCAUST MEMORIAL, 1981 (BELOW). Elbert Weinberg (1928–1991) was a noted artist and educator. He took art classes at the Hartford Art School of the Wadsworth Atheneum and studied with German sculptor Henry Kreis. Weinberg was the youngest recipient of the Prix de Rome, which enabled him to spend two years in Italy. He also received a Guggenheim Fellowship and taught at several universities. In 1988, he was commissioned to create a sculpture for Art For All, a public art project sponsored by the *Hartford Courant*. Weinberg created the 16-foot-high Holocaust Memorial at the Mandell Jewish Community Center, which depicts two raised arms holding a *shofar* (ram's horn) and forming the Hebrew word *chai* (life). The statue, commissioned by local Holocaust survivors David Chase and Simon Konover, was dedicated in 1981.

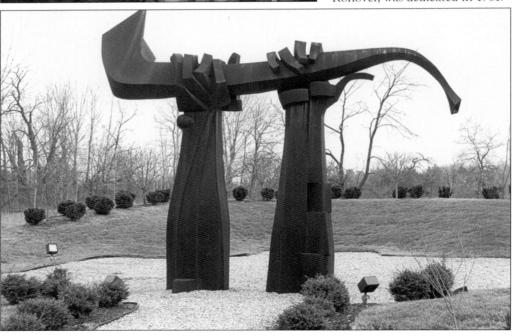

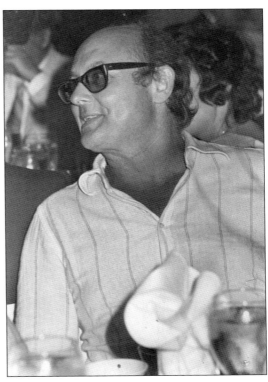

Sol LeWitt, 1960s. Sol LeWitt (1928–2007) was born in Hartford and raised in New Britain. He took art classes at the Wadsworth Atheneum and received a BFA degree from Syracuse University. He spent several years as a graphic designer, doing paste-ups and mechanicals for *Seventeen* magazine and for the noted architect I.M. Pei. In the late 1960s, LeWitt became famous for his wall drawings and is considered one of the founders of both minimal and conceptual art. In the 1980s, he moved from New York City to Spoleto, Italy, and later relocated to Chester, Connecticut. Throughout his life, he assisted younger artists and was considered a patron and friend by his many colleagues. (Both, courtesy of the LeWitt Collection.)

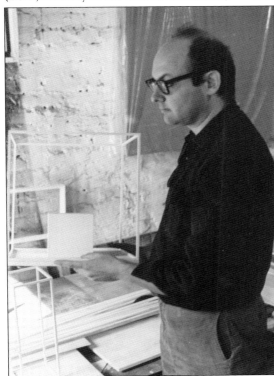

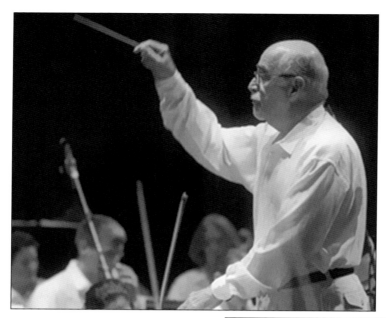

JACK ELLIOTT, C. 1990S. Born Irwin Elliott Zucker in Hartford, Jack Elliott (1927–2001) grew up in West Hartford and graduated from what is now the Hartt School of Music in 1951. He became a successful Hollywood composer and arranger and worked with stars including Judy Garland and Julie Andrews. He was also the musical director for many awards shows, including a 30-year run with the Grammys. (Courtesy of Alan Elliott.)

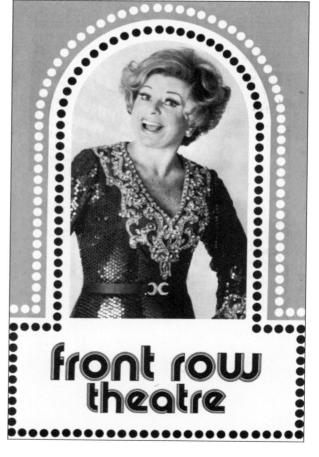

TOTIE FIELDS, 1978. Totie Fields (1927–1978), born Sophie Feldman, was a comedian in the 1960s and 1970s and got her big break on *The Ed Sullivan Show*. She was a frequent guest on daytime variety shows. Despite health problems, Fields performed in nightclubs and on television. She was voted Entertainer of the Year and Female Comedy Star of the Year by the American Guild of Variety Artists in 1978.

Eight

SPORTS

Although times were difficult for early immigrants and their families, many children found an outlet in organized sports, either in school or through local organizations like the YMHA and YWHA. The first branch of the YMHA was established in 1878 by German Jews who wanted recreational opportunities for their children. Although this effort did not succeed, two other YMHA groups were later created. In 1891, the Hartford Hebrew Association was opened to provide these services to new immigrants, and another YMHA for all immigrants and their children opened in 1915. Also in 1915, Annie Fisher, a prominent local educator, founded a YWHA for girls and young women. Due to the Depression, these organizations had to close in the late 1930s, but they were replaced by the Jewish Center Association in the early 1940s. Eventually, as the Jewish Community Center grew and expanded, a number of competitive and recreational sports teams were formed, and the JCC became the site for organized sports. They also sponsored teams that participated in local, national, and international competitions such as the Maccabi Games.

Hartford's high schools also had strong teams, which did well on the local and regional level. Many participants went on to play on a college level, having been stand-out performers in high school. Not only did Jews take part in a number of sports, but several owned minor league or semiprofessional teams, bringing a variety of sports to local fans.

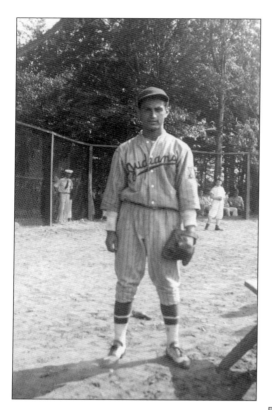

J. Sydney Greenbaum, c. 1935. J. Sydney Greenbaum (1909–1984) graduated from Weaver High School, where he ran track. He played on the Connecticut Kings softball team and also played football. In addition, he was the chairman of a tennis tournament at Keney Park. Greenbaum was also the executive director of the Bess and Paul Sigel Hebrew Academy for a time.

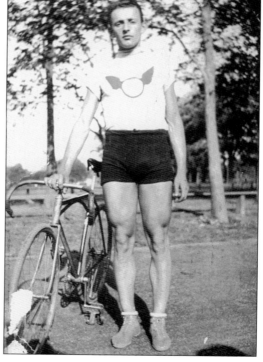

Louis B. Rogow, 1920s. Born in Russia, Rogow (1887–1991) was a bicycle racer and ice skater who won the state championship in bicycle racing seven times. He qualified for the Olympics in 1920 and also set a world record for a 26-mile race. In addition, he was a city ice-skating champion. Rogow founded the Birken Manufacturing Company in 1943 and created the Rogow-Birken Foundation, offering scholarships to engineering students.

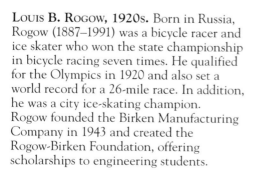

MANUEL "MANNY" LEIBERT, 1997. At age 18, Manny Leibert (c. 1913–2011), left, began coaching and promoting Hartford athletes. After boxing had been banned in Connecticut for eight years, he helped revive it in 1973. Leibert served as the president of the Connecticut Boxing Guild, managed and promoted amateur boxers, and promoted professional boxing and wrestling matches for 50 years. He was inducted into the Connecticut Boxing Hall of Fame in 2006.

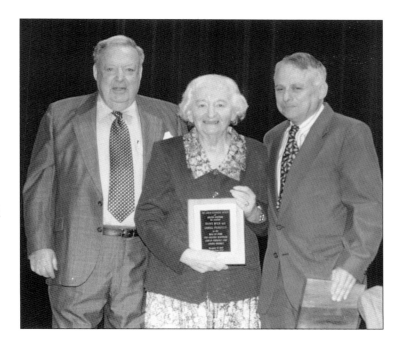

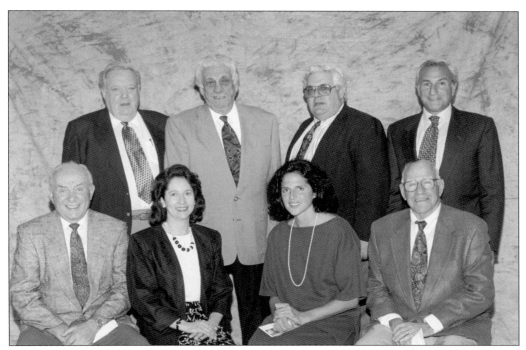

HALL OF FAME FOR GREATER HARTFORD JEWISH ATHLETES, 1995. In 1983, the Jewish Historical Society of Greater Hartford created a hall of fame to honor the contributions of adult Jewish athletes in the Greater Hartford area. It was designed to be a permanent record of the accomplishments of these notable athletes. Manny Liebert (second row, far left) and Stanley Weisen (first row, far right) were cochairs of the Hall of Fame for Greater Hartford Jewish Athletes.

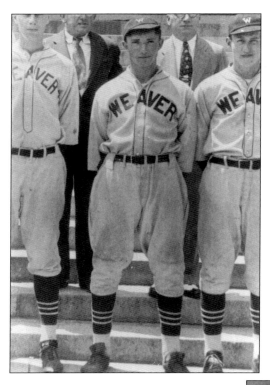

DR. IRVING "CHICK" WALTMAN, 1933. Dr. Chick Waltman (1915–2016), center, attended Weaver High School, where he played football, basketball, and baseball. He was class president and salutatorian and won an award as best athlete with the best academic record. Dr. Waltman played baseball and swam at Amherst College and graduated from Yale University Medical School. He became a surgeon and was the first Jewish doctor on the medical staff at Hartford Hospital.

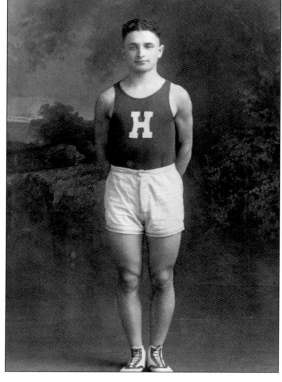

IRVING JOSEPH, 1920. Irving Joseph (1904–1951) graduated from Hartford High School, where he ran track and was co-captain of the team. As a junior in 1920, he set a world record for the 20-yard dash, a standard event at the time, gaining state and national acclaim. At Syracuse University, he set a record for the 60-yard dash. After law school, he practiced in the Hartford area and became a judge in Bristol.

KID KAPLAN, 1926 (RIGHT) AND C. 1930S (BELOW). Louis "Kid" Kaplan (1902–1970) was born in Russia and came to Meriden, Connecticut, as a child. He started boxing in self-defense, and his professional boxing career began at age 19. He won the World Featherweight Boxing Championship in 1925. He then became a successful lightweight, but could not find an opponent for a title match. Kaplan was called the "Meriden Buzz Saw" for his aggressive style, but he was also known for his courage and integrity, especially after turning down a gangster's offer of $50,000 to throw a fight. He took pride in being Jewish and wore a Jewish star on his trunks. After he retired in 1933, he settled in Hartford and became a restaurateur. He coached youngsters and refereed boxing matches. Kaplan was inducted into the International Boxing Hall of Fame in 2003.

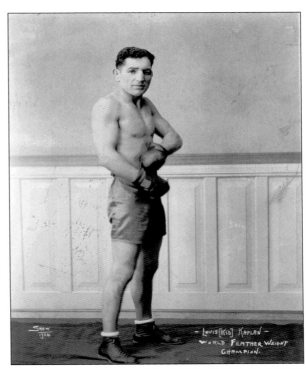

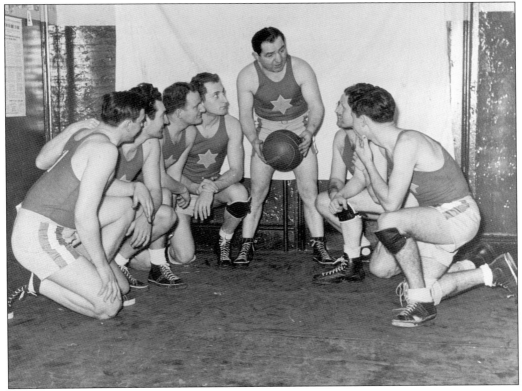

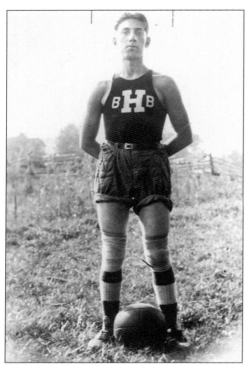

DR. MORRIS COHEN, 1914. Morris Cohen (1899–1988) was born in Russia and came to the United States in 1900. He played basketball and football in high school and graduated from Tufts University. He also played for professional teams in Boston before returning to Hartford to open a dental practice. In Hartford, Dr. Cohen played for the local championship YMHA team and also coached both men's and women's basketball teams.

DR. MORRIS COHEN YOUTH ATHLETIC AWARD, 1989. This award was established in 1989 by Dr. Cohen's family and the Jewish Historical Society of Greater Hartford in recognition of Dr. Cohen's civic and athletic contributions to the community. This award is presented to Jewish high school students who have excelled in sports, scholarship, and leadership.

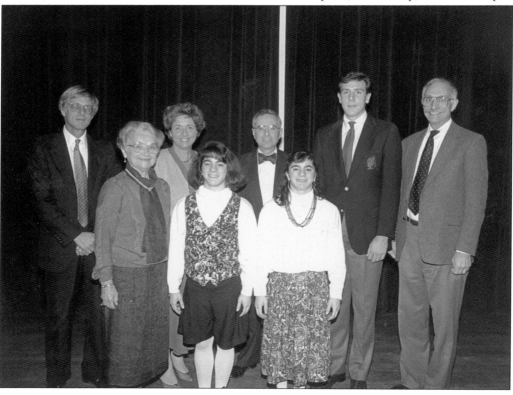

JOSEPH "JOE" DUNN, C. 1917. Joe Dunn (1899–1968) was the first Jewish captain of the Hartford High School football team and led the team to an undefeated season in 1917. He went on to play at Boston University and graduated from the Massachusetts College of Pharmacy and Boston University Law School. Injuries ended his sports career. He later became a businessman and community philanthropist.

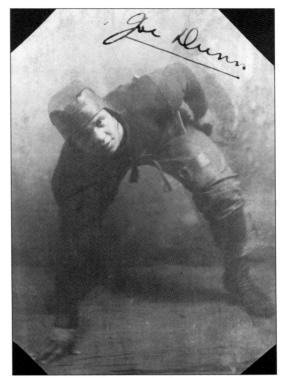

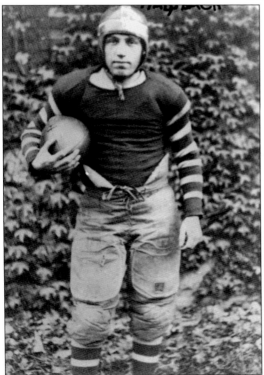

REUBEN COHEN, C. 1910S. Reuben Cohen (1899–1970) was considered one of the city's best athletes. He played three sports at Hartford High School: football, basketball, and baseball. After college, he played for part of one season with the St. Louis Cardinals baseball team under the name "Reuben Ewing." Returning to Hartford, he captained the YMHA basketball team for two years and won the city championship in 1923.

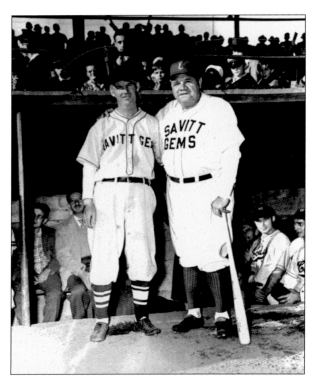

SAVITT GEMS MANAGER JIGGER
FARRELL WITH BABE RUTH, 1945.
The Gems were a semiprofessional
baseball team formed in the 1920s
by William Savitt, a jeweler. He
owned Bulkeley Stadium from 1932
to 1946 and brought in stars such
as Babe Ruth and Ted Williams for
exhibition games, with proceeds
going to charity. Before baseball's
integration, Savitt invited all-black
teams with outstanding athletes like
Roy Campanella to play against the
Gems. (Courtesy of Bob Farrell.)

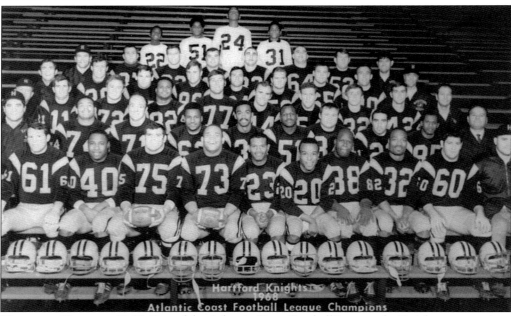

HARTFORD KNIGHTS, 1968. Part of the Atlantic Coast Football League, the Knights were a minor
league team owned by Marvin "Pete" Savin. As a semiprofessional team, most of the players held
other jobs, but many hoped for an opportunity to join the NFL or AFL. The Knights played at
Dillon Stadium for six years and had an undefeated season in 1972. The team disbanded in 1974.
(Courtesy of Bill Ryczek.)

Sylvia Greenbaum Novarr, 1944. For seven consecutive years, Sylvia Novarr (1923–2014) was the Hartford Public Parks women's tennis champion, and for five consecutive years, she won the New England Women's Public Parks Tennis Championship. She was the first female athlete inducted into the Jewish Historical Society of Greater Hartford's Sports Hall of Fame.

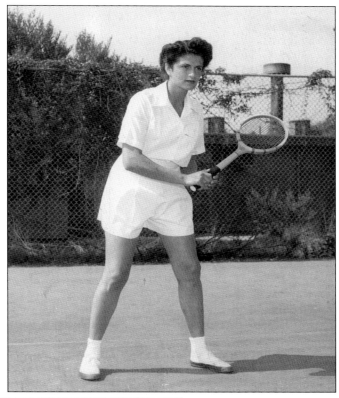

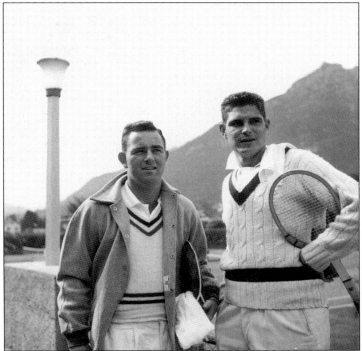

Gerald "Gerry" Slobin, 1950s. Gerry Slobin (1932–2001), left, graduated from Weaver High School in 1950. He excelled at basketball, football, and particularly tennis, and was the undefeated Class A single's champion from 1948 to 1950, the highest ranked tennis player in New England. Slobin attended the University of Miami on a tennis scholarship and became a professional player and promoter. He later opened the Bloomfield Racquet Club, the state's first indoor tennis facility.

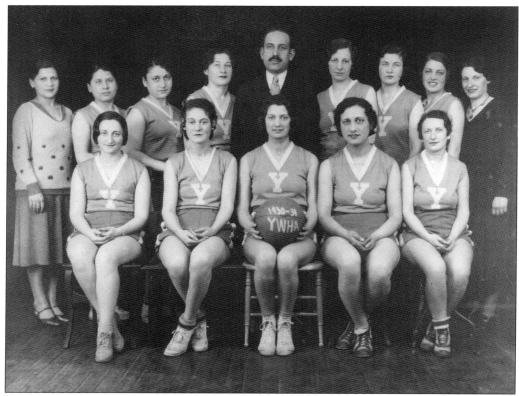

YWHA BASKETBALL, 1930–1931. The Young Women's Hebrew Association basketball teams played in the 1920s and 1930s in the Hartford County Women's League, which included the YWCA, Aetna Life, and teams from Simsbury. Dr. Morris Cohen managed the women's and men's teams. The YWHA did not have its own gym facility, so practices were held in local YWCAs or area schools.

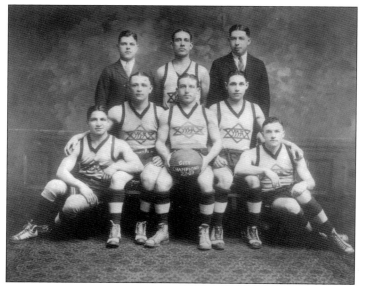

YMHA BASKETBALL, 1922–1923. The Young Men's Hebrew Association basketball team won several city championships in the early 1920s, playing teams all over Connecticut and Massachusetts. The team did not have its own gymnasium, so they played at several locations, including Hartford Public High School and Foot Guard Hall. Team members often faced anti-Semitic slurs from spectators but still had a large base of loyal fans who faithfully attended games.

HARRIET J. NOVARR, c. 1975. Harriet Novarr (1956–2002) played varsity volleyball, badminton, and baseball at Hartford Public High School in the early 1970s before attending Syracuse University on the school's first women's basketball scholarship. She played professionally in Israel and the United States, participating in the United States' first women's league. She later joined the Washington Tennis Foundation, a non-profit organization supporting junior tennis in the Washington, DC, area.

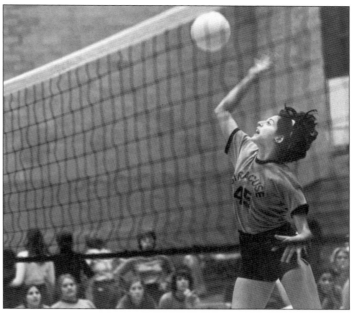

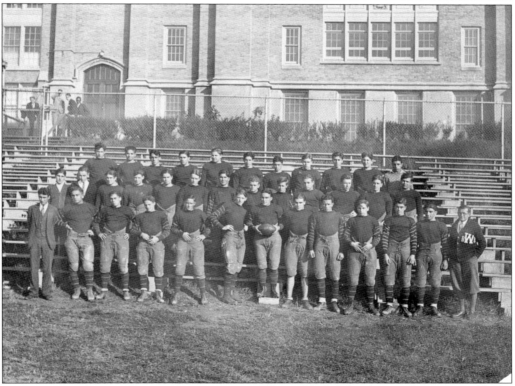

WEAVER HIGH SCHOOL FOOTBALL, 1924–1928. Weaver High School opened in 1924 and had a football team nearly from its inception, with its first win coming in October 1924. Many Jewish athletes at Weaver were on the football team in addition to their participation in other sports such as basketball and track.

BIBLIOGRAPHY

Dalin, David G., and Jonathan Rosenbaum. *Making a Life, Building a Community: A History of the Jews of Hartford*. New York, NY: Holmes & Meier, 1997.

Hoffman, Betty N. *Honoring the Past: Building the Future: The History of the Jewish Federation of Greater Hartford*. Hartford, CT: Jewish Historical Society of Greater Hartford, 2007.

Silverman, Morris. *Hartford Jews 1659–1970*. Hartford, CT: Connecticut Historical Society, 1970.

Sutherland, John, and Marsha Lotstein, eds. *1843–1943, One Hundred Years of Jewish Congregations in Connecticut: An Architectural Survey; Connecticut Jewish History: Volume 2, Number 1*. Hartford, CT: Jewish Historical Society of Greater Hartford, 1991.

Walden, Joan, ed. *Remembering the Old Neighborhood: Stories from Hartford's North End*. Hartford, CT: Jewish Historical Society of Greater Hartford, 2009.

—————. *Revisiting our Neighborhoods: Stories From Hartford's Past*. Hartford, CT: Jewish Historical Society of Greater Hartford, 2013.

About the Organization

The Jewish Historical Society of Greater Hartford, a beneficiary agency of the Jewish Federation of Greater Hartford, is dedicated to the collection and preservation of historical documents, photographs, oral histories, and memorabilia of Hartford's Jewish community. The society seeks to reach the largest audience possible through publications, exhibitions, workshops, and educational programs.

The society was founded as a nonprofit organization in 1971 by a dedicated group of individuals who realized the importance of documenting the life and history of the Jewish community. It has since evolved into a respected archival center visited by researchers, authors, and academics. Hundreds of participants have attended the society's educational and cultural programs, exhibitions, and tours. There are now over 700 members, and membership continues to grow. Please visit www.jhsgh.org for more information about the society and to view its online historical exhibits.

DISCOVER THOUSANDS OF LOCAL HISTORY BOOKS FEATURING MILLIONS OF VINTAGE IMAGES

Arcadia Publishing, the leading local history publisher in the United States, is committed to making history accessible and meaningful through publishing books that celebrate and preserve the heritage of America's people and places.

Find more books like this at
www.arcadiapublishing.com

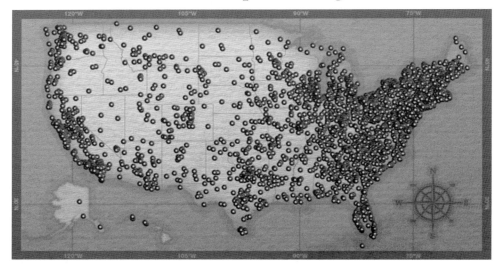

Search for your hometown history, your old stomping grounds, and even your favorite sports team.

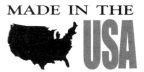